# All New Real-Life Case Studies for School Administrators

## William Hayes

ROWMAN & LITTLEFIELD EDUCATION
Lanham • New York • Toronto • Plymouth, UK

Published in the United States of America
by Rowman & Littlefield Education
A Division of Rowman & Littlefield Publishers, Inc.
A wholly owned subsidiary of The Rowman & Littlefield Publishing Group, Inc.
4501 Forbes Boulevard, Suite 200, Lanham, Maryland 20706
www.rowmaneducation.com

Estover Road
Plymouth PL6 7PY
United Kingdom

British Library Cataloguing in Publication Information Available

**Library of Congress Cataloging-in-Publication Data**

Hayes, William, 1938–
　　All new real-life case studies for school administrators / William Hayes.
　　　　p. cm.
　　Includes bibliographical references.
　　ISBN-13: 978-1-57886-679-3 (cloth : alk. paper)
　　ISBN-10: 1-57886-679-0 (cloth : alk. paper)
　　ISBN-13: 978-1-57886-680-9 (pbk. : alk. paper)
　　ISBN-10: 1-57886-680-4 (pbk. : alk. paper)
　1. School management and organization—United States—Case studies. 2. School
administrators—United States—Case studies. I. Title.
　　LB2806.H384 2007
　　371.200973—dc22

2007027897

∞™ The paper used in this publication meets the minimum requirements of American
National Standard for Information Sciences—Permanence of Paper for Printed Library
Materials, ANSI/NISO Z39.48-1992.
Manufactured in the United States of America.

# Contents

# Foreword

What does it mean to be a principal? How is it different from being a teacher? Does an administrator need to know more or think differently from a teacher? Can I be successful as a school leader? These are typical questions asked by teachers considering a move into school administration. These are also questions that are not easily answered. Future school administrators need to deal with questions like these as they prepare for a career in educational leadership. In the process of seeking administrative certification, we are always thankful when we find a book that can help us to develop our knowledge, skills, and attitudes related to the roles we seek. One such book is this new work by William Hayes.

In the pages that follow, Hayes provides current case studies of problematic situations faced by school administrators today. Improvement of reading scores, bullying, high-stakes testing, and dealing with difficult people are but a few of the new topics in this update of his 1999 book of case studies. The new volume contains additional information related to each case study presented in the book including a list of additional sources that can be very useful to instructors and students.

Public school administrators face difficult choices on a daily basis. As an assistant superintendent for curriculum and instruction for a large suburban school district in New York, my days were dominated by what I came to call "the tyranny of the urge." Most often the problems we administrators face each day present us with true dilemmas. Experienced administrators would agree that it is often the little issues that come at you quickly that, if not handled well, can come back to haunt you. By definition a dilemma does not have a single answer that will work best in every situation, so we must be prepared to use information gathering, observational, and critical thinking skills on a daily basis to understand and try to solve the problems facing us. This is exactly the approach to problem-solving found in Hayes' new book.

Americans have become accustomed to television shows that present topics "ripped from the headlines." Likewise, Hayes has used his many years of experience in schools as a teacher, department chair, principal, and superintendent of schools to guide the selection of studies in this volume. The cases are timely and reflect the incredible breadth of issues that administrators tackle in today's schools.

The post-Columbine era has made the issue of school safety an enormous concern for school leaders. How do we ensure that our schools are safe for all? Can our schools be safe without turning them into prisons? How do we balance the need for security with our desire to have our schools be welcoming to parents and community members? These are the type of questions that are engendered by one case study in Hayes' new book. This topic can help future administrators contemplate some of the difficult choices that have to be made.

No single book could possibly prepare a new administrator for every situation that she or he will face. Hayes' book does not try to do this. Instead, this collection of stories about life in schools attempts to engender in the new educational leader a "habit of the mind." That habit would be to collect all available information on a given situation and carefully consider all sides of the issue before deciding on a course of action. Having carefully thought through a particular problem before we make our decisions can also make it easier for us to explain our decisions. Others may not agree with us, but at least they will know that our action was based on careful decision making. We cannot always be right, but we can be thoughtful, considerate, and judicious.

One way to help prepare people who are seeking administrative certification is through the use of high-quality case studies that present current, real dilemmas. This book does just that. *All New Real-Life Case Studies for School Administrators* offers a meaningful collection of stories and analyses that will elicit thoughtful reflection on both the cases being considered and the essential attitudes needed to be a successful public school administrator in today's schools.

Dr. Gary P. DeBolt
Retired, Assistant Superintendent
for Curriculum and Instruction
Fairport Central School District
Fairport, NY

# Acknowledgments

There are several people to thank for their help in preparing this book. To identify subjects for the case studies, I have had many conversations with family, friends, and colleagues. In fact, there were so many people involved in that process that it is impossible to name them all or even to remember where the initial ideas originated. Among family, I have talked to my grandchildren, Mike and Laura, their mother, Beth, and their aunt, Linda. Two of my children, Jennifer and Matt, also provided input. I won't even try to mention all of the current and retired school administrators with whom I have talked for fear that I will leave someone out.

I had three essential partners in completing this project. Linda Jones, who is our college's director of reference and bibliographic instruction, was responsible for all of the supplementary reference material that is at the end of each case study. These sources are new features, which were not present in my previous case study books. There is no question in my mind that they enhance the book in that they provide sources that will be helpful to both professors and students using the book. Linda has spent many hours selecting sources that relate directly to the cases, and I am grateful to her for making this feature possible in the book.

Nicole Stoodley is a senior in the Roberts Wesleyan College Art Education Program. Along with typing the entire book, Nicole has been actively involved in every phase of the project. As a recent high school graduate, she has helped to identify problems for cases and assisted in making them as realistic as possible. In addition, she helped to edit the text and was the source of most of the names for the characters. Nicole is a very talented young person who will be a wonderful teacher. This book would not have been possible without Nicole.

Finally, I thank my wife, Nancy, who has read every page of all of my eleven books. In doing so, she has always found errors that I have made and has also contributed valuable suggestions. I am grateful for her assistance, along with her patience for the many hours I spend with these books.

# Introduction

In 1999, when I decided to write a book titled *Real-Life Case Studies for School Administrators*, I hoped that such a text would prove useful to professors teaching classes in the field of school administration. The case study method was already an important teaching method being used in fields such as law, business, medicine, and social work. Since its publication in the year 2000, the book has been used at colleges and universities across the country. Apparently the issues raised in the case studies were ones that were helpful in preparing future school administrators.

Unlike most textbooks, which give the students information and provide answers for future examinations, case studies are open-ended. Usually there are numerous approaches to dealing with a complex set of circumstances. In the classroom, professors are able to elicit from their students varied responses. This creates a classroom atmosphere that engages students and forces them to think like school administrators. In many ways, such classes are more helpful to students than merely being exposed to the thoughts of a professor and a textbook. Many students actually prefer this type of teaching and learning.

After recently reviewing the cases included in this earlier edition, it became clear to me that many of the problems facing school administrators today did not exist in 1999. This realization, along with the fact that many of the cases in this first book were based on incidents that had occurred as much as a quarter of a century earlier, led me to conclude that the time was right for a new book containing more up-to-date cases. These new cases deal with such topics as the No Child Left Behind Act and the increased need for school security policies. A plethora of new concerns has emerged for school leaders, and I hope that a text dealing with these issues will be useful to many teachers and students.

With these goals in mind, I carried on a series of conversations with current and recently retired school administrators. Using their input, I developed this book, providing an entirely new group of dilemmas that confront school administrators. Given that many instructors use case studies in introductory administration courses, I have included situations that will be appropriate for classes that contain students with a variety of administrative ambitions. Although my first case study book dealt primarily with problems facing principals and superintendents, this volume also includes situations that department heads, athletic directors, assistant principals, assistant superintendents, and special education chairpersons might face.

Another difference is that the cases come from a variety of school districts. There are problems that might arise in urban communities as well as suburban and rural districts. I believe that this approach can help to acquaint future administrators with a more comprehensive group of challenges that they are likely to encounter in their careers.

Another new feature included in this book is a short bibliography relating to the subject of each case study. These sources offer faculty and students the opportunity to do additional research on the topic dealt with in each case. It is my hope that the cases included in this book will help increase the realism of administration programs and that an even larger number of teachers and students will benefit from discussing these scenarios.

*Case Study 1*

# Should We Get Rid
# of Our Middle Schools?

*restructuring a district*

**The first junior high school (school for grades seven, eight, and nine) was opened in 1909 in Columbus, Ohio. Junior high schools, based on the same model as public high schools (grades ten through twelve or nine through twelve), sprang up quickly throughout the nation. This was especially true in larger school districts. By the mid-1960s, books and articles in educational journals were calling for a school district organization plan that provided a more effective transition for students in the middle grades. The idea spread quickly, and by the end of the twentieth century there were already twelve thousand middle schools (grades five through eight or grades six through eight). More recently, the middle school model has come under fire by critics who question the lack of academic progress of many middle school students. This case study deals with such criticism that erupted in one school district.**

Dr. Renee DeYoung, superintendent of the Jackson City School District, had just read the article in the *New York Times* for the third time. It had been brought in that day by George Davis, the newest member of the Jackson Board of Education, who said he was just passing by the district office and wanted to talk with Dr. DeYoung. He began their conversation by referring to her report on test scores given at the previous board meeting. George said he had been concerned because, although the test scores of the students in grades three through five had shown improvement, the results in the middle school were disappointing in that there had been a decline in each of the past three years. It was these poor results that had caused his interest in the newspaper article he had given her.

With the headline "Taking Middle Schools Out of the Middle," the *Times* reporter had written about what she called, "a national effort to rethink middle schools." The article suggested that this reassessment was occurring because of an "increasingly well-documented" slump in the test scores of middle school children. Additional impetus to the trend was also coming because of the "middle school crime rates and stubborn high school drop out rates." For some of those concerned with the trends, the answer was to "get rid of middle schools entirely." The article went on to suggest that the critics were divided on what type of school organization should replace middle schools. Historically, a middle school consists of grades six, seven, and eight or possibly five, six, seven, and eight and one group or critics believed that children ages eleven through thirteen should remain sheltered in the "nurturing cocoon of the elementary school."

An organization that featured a K–8 school would postpone, until the children had matured, the move to a more impersonal secondary school. Having the same teacher or perhaps two teachers in a self-contained setting would add to the sense of security of these students. The article cited the initiative of Paul Vella, the chief executive of the Philadelphia City Schools, who "has closed seventeen traditional middle schools since 2002, while converting some three dozen elementary schools into K–8s."

Other critics of middle school mentioned in the *Times* article felt that, "11, 12, and 13 year-olds thrive in the presence of older role models." In New York City, there are now thirty-eight grade six through twelve schools. Renee knew that in a city not far from the Jackson District, middle schools had been abandoned for a grade seven through twelve organizational pattern.

George had been so impressed by the article that he had already had a conversation with another board member, Jim Streeter. Both of these men had a personal interest in middle schools because they had children who were currently in the fourth grade. As a result of their talk, they wanted an item placed on the agenda at the next board meeting, which they had labeled, "The Formation of a Task Force to Consider the Restructuring of Our Schools." Their goal was to have the board establish a group of administrators, teachers, and parents to study the issue. They made the additional suggestion that some students be included on the committee, which would report its recommendations to the board. Taken aback by the request, Renee had asked George to give her at least a month to research the issue. Despite his enthusiasm for immediate action, he had agreed to put off the discussion for one month.

As a former assistant superintendent in the district, who had been instrumental in establishing the four middle schools, Renee had earned a reputation as a middle school advocate. During the late 1980s, she had published articles arguing for the need for schools that could provide a smooth transition for children passing from the security of small elementary schools with self-contained classes into the impersonal atmosphere of traditional high schools. With the support of administrators, teachers, and many parents, the district converted the district's four junior high schools into middle schools. At the time, Renee was convinced that the junior highs, which housed grades seven, eight, and nine, were merely mini-high schools. The schedules, teaching methods, and even the social events in the junior highs were almost identical to those in the high schools.

During that same period, the state Education Department strongly supported the formation of middle schools. A separate teaching certificate was created for those teachers wishing to work at this level. Among other classes, future middle school teachers were required to take courses such as middle school theory. In this class, they learned about the physical and social development of middle school students. They also would be taught about teaching methods that might appeal to these children. Teachers were encouraged to lecture less and include more lessons that used "hands-on" experiences and group activities.

National and state middle school organizations for teachers and administrators emerged and actively published their own periodicals for educators at this level. The middle school movement that Renee had supported urged schools to substitute activity nights for the typical junior high or high school dance. Such an event might feature volleyball and board games and would replace the dances, which featured dimly lit rooms and loud music. The proponents of middle schools urged more emphasis on intramurals while downplaying interscholastic sports. If the middle school had a basketball team, frequently there would be a league rule that all participants had the opportunity to play at least one quarter of the game.

Academically, emphasis was given to integrating various curriculum areas and project-based learning. Middle school educators were urged to think about the "whole child" and consider students' emotional, intellectual, and physical well-being. Schools would implement efforts to strengthen parents' involvement in their students' educations. A middle school's organizational pattern might also vary from the traditional junior high approach. At the sixth grade level, students might continue to work with only one or two teachers. Even when the seventh and eight graders began to travel to different classrooms for each subject, the teachers at those grade levels would work as a team. There would be a concerted effort for teachers to get to know students as individuals, and counseling services would be available to all children. In many schools, advisement periods would be part of the schedule, allowing students time to converse with a faculty member. Efforts were made to maintain a high level of school spirit as teachers and administrators organized and staged various projects and events to foster unity within the student body.

Renee remembered that in her first administrative job, she worked as an assistant middle school principal in another district. As a still fairly young person, she had become highly involved in the school's "Spirit Week," a series of activity nights, and "dress down" days. She still kept a picture taken of herself dressed as a scarecrow at the middle school Halloween party in her office. Unfortunately, she had to admit to herself that sometimes this type of activity might have overshadowed academics in the school. Perhaps it was this emphasis on making school more pleasant for these students that was responsible for the increased criticism of the middle school movement during recent years. She knew that there were those who thought that middle schools were so concerned with issues such as the student's self-esteem, that not enough stress was placed on academic learning.

Although she could accept the validity of some of the complaints, the thought of abandoning her district's middle schools depressed her. Many of the older faculty members who had joined her in supporting the change from junior high schools would undoubtedly feel the same. On the other hand, she had several teachers on her faculty, who were former high school teachers and who had never become comfortable with the more laid back middle school environment.

As she thought about the alternatives of either a K through eight or seven through twelve school, Renee saw drawbacks in both of these schemes. At the same time, she knew that somehow the four middle schools in her district needed to boost their students' scores on the mandated standardized tests. She knew it must be possible, as there were many middle schools in the state that had decent test scores, and they were accomplishing this without restructuring their school system. It was her challenge during the next month to prepare for the now inevitable discussion that might lead to such a restructuring in the Jackson City School District.

## DISCUSSION QUESTIONS

1. Why do you think the standardized test results of middle school students in America are often disappointing?
2. If a district were to abandon the middle school model, would you favor a K through eighth school or a grade seven through twelve school? Why?
3. Are there any specific ways you might suggest to improve the test results in our middle schools without resorting to a new organizational pattern?
4. What should Renee do about the board members' idea to form a task force to consider a restructuring of the school system?

## ADDITIONAL RESOURCES

Bedard, Kelly, and Chau Do. 2005. "Are Middle Schools More Effective? The Impact of School Structure on Student Outcomes." *Journal of Human Resources* 40 (3): 660–682.

Dembo, Myron H., and Martin J. Eaton. 2000. "Self-Regulation of Academic Learning in Middle-Level Schools." *Elementary School Journal* 100 (5): 473–490.

Fischer, Max W. 2003. "Are Middle Schools Getting a Bum Rap?" Voice of Experience. *Education World.* March 15, 2007. http://www.educationworld.com/a_curr/profdev052.shtml

Gable, R. A., Hester, P. P., Hester, L. R., Hendrickson, J. M., and Sze, S. 2005. "Cognitive, Affective, and Relational dimensions of Middle School Students: Implications for Improving Discipline and Instruction." *Clearing House* 79 (September/October): 40–44.

Gootman, Elissa. "Taking the Middle Schoolers Out of the Middle." *New York Times*, January 24, 2007, A1.

Juvonen, J., Le, V.-N., Kaganoff, T., Augustine, C., and Constant, L. 2004. *Focus on the Wonder Years: Challenges Facing the American Middle School.* March 15, 2007. http://www.rand.org/pubs/monographs/2004/RAND_MG139.pdf.

Manzo, Kathleen Kennedy. 2001. "Academic Rigor Urged in Middle Schools." *Gifted Child Today* 24 (2): 8–9.

Strahan, David B., and Krystal Layell. 2006. "Connecting Caring and Action through Responsive Teaching: How One Team Accomplished Success in a Struggling Middle School." *Clearing House* 79 (January/February): 147–153.

*Case Study 2*

# The Best Candidate

## *site-based management*

**Teacher involvement in school decision making is not a new concept. Sometimes called "site-based management," the practice is based on the assumption that those individuals working in a school building are in the best position to make decisions that directly affect that school. In addition, the theory argues that if people take part in making a decision, they are more apt to support a course of action. Of course, like any other innovation site-based decision making can create new problems. Sometimes it complicates decision making by creating another layer in the hierarchy. This can result in prolonging the process by increasing the time it takes to reach a consensus. Furthermore, many decisions legally require the approval of the superintendent and the board of education. There is also the possibility of additional conflict especially if a principal disagrees with the recommendations of faculty members.**

When the new superintendent, Dr. Nicole Stoodley, began her tenure in the Malone City School District, she introduced a number of innovative procedures and policies. One of her ideas was proving to have a far-reaching impact on the district's personnel policies. After several meetings with the district's union president, Erika Crow, a joint memo signed by the superintendent and the union president was circulated in every building in the district.

Dr. Sam Sadker, the previous superintendent, had been a rather autocratic individual who was constantly involved in conflicts with the teachers' union. It did not help that Erika Crow, the union president, was a stubborn and outspoken critic of the superintendent. She also was a skilled negotiator who loved to argue with the superintendent and even board members. As part of the hiring process, the new superintendent had been fully informed of the history of the conflict between the district and the teachers' union. The school board made it clear to Nicole that it was seeking peace and that it was depending on her to bring it about. The agreement announced in the joint memo stated that in the future, the teachers in each school would have "significant input" in decisions involving personnel and the expenditure of money budgeted for that school building.

John Stacy had served as an assistant superintendent for personnel in the district for nine years. He had worked under three superintendents. Each of them had their own management style, but all of them had given to the personnel office, which John managed, significant authority in hiring and supervision of professional personnel, union negotiations, and contract enforcement. Until Sam Sadker's tenure, the arrangement seemed to work effectively. Unfortunately, during the past three years, there had been numerous issues involving personnel that caused grievances and even picketing at board of education meetings. Although he was aware that the new superintendent was having private discussions with the union president, John was disappointed that he was not invited to participate in these conversations. He was very surprised when Nicole announced at an administrative meeting that teacher committees would be involved in the selection of all new personnel in the future.

In the past, his office had screened all of the applications and selected candidates who would be invited to the district office for an interview. After John had screened and interviewed these candidates, he would select three who would then be asked to interview with the building principals. In some of the schools, the principals might ask an assistant principal, a department chairperson, or a grade-level chairperson to participate in the building interview. Other principals would interview the candidate alone and work directly with the assistant superintendent to decide on their choice of the new faculty member. Of course, this selection had to be then approved by the superintendent and the board of education. During his nine years as assistant superintendent, John had never had one of his recommendations overturned by either the superintendent or the board.

Jim O'Connor was one of the principals who had chosen not to include others in the interview process. Of all the schools in the district, his was perhaps the one in which the principal exercised the most power. Needless to say, he was not happy when he was told that the teachers in his school would now be allowed to participate in the interviews of at least three teacher candidates when there was a vacancy at their grade level. The grade-level team members would then prepare a recommendation of the candidates in the order of the priority that they established. Not only would they be allowed to interview the candidates, but the new policy allowed them to review all of the eligible applications. If they felt it was appropriate, a person other than those selected by the assistant superintendent for personnel could be added to the interview list. It was this provision in the new policy that caused the current dilemma.

After John sent the applications and resumes of three outstanding candidates to the schools, the fourth grade team at Jim's school asked to review all of the elementary school teacher applications. After looking at dozens of files, they informed Jim that they wished to have a fourth name added to the interview list. As part of the process, John had carefully checked the references of the three candidates he had selected and all of them were enthusiastically endorsed by those people he contacted. Of course this was not unusual, as candidates were unlikely to list people who would say anything unfavorable.

As a veteran personnel officer, John always went beyond the list of references and talked to his own friends and acquaintances who might know the candidates. He was a personal friend of several teacher education professors at the local colleges who might have taught some of the candidates. If the applicant was from a neighboring district, he would call contacts in those districts who would usually give him an unbiased opinion about the candidates. The three individuals he had chosen as applicants had been thoroughly checked out, and he was confident they were all outstanding candidates.

One in particular, Cindy Stores had already taught fourth grade for three years in a district similar to the Malone City School District. Her principal said that she was the best teacher on his faculty and that he was very sad about losing her. The principal told John that Cindy was moving to Malone because her husband had just taken an important management position in the largest bank in the city.

A careful administrator, John naturally wished to give the same scrutiny to the candidate recommended by the fourth grade team. He was surprised to find the name of one of the fourth grade teachers listed as a reference. Further investigation turned up the fact that the recommended candidate, Betty White, had regularly substituted at the fourth-grade level at the Horace Mann Elementary School, where Jim was principal. There was little doubt that the interview team was well acquainted with Betty. In talking with her other references, there was general agreement that Betty was a "nice person" whom everybody seemed to like. Her college transcript, however, was average, and her professors reported that she was a B– student who seemed to be quite popular with her peers. The evaluations written by her master teachers during student teaching rated her as being above average but not outstanding.

With the numerous excellent elementary school applicants he had to choose from, John concluded that had the teachers not chosen to interview Betty, he would not have recommended her for a final interview. When he shared his findings with Jim, he learned that Betty was a personal friend of three of the four fourth grade teachers at Horace Mann Elementary. Two of them were active with her at the same church and another was a member of her bowling team. It appeared that the current fourth grade team had really enjoyed the days when Betty had substituted at their grade level. John also learned that there had been lunchroom conversations about the possibility that when Kay Dermity retired Betty might be a great replacement.

After the principal and the team interviewed the four candidates, John was not surprised that the priority list submitted placed Betty as the number one choice. What was shocking was that Cindy, who was the favorite of both Jim and John, was number four on the list. The principal was incensed by the recommendation and suggested that this overt cronyism was like the "old boys network," although the teachers were fairly young women. In Jim's opinion, Betty was the last choice, and Cindy was by far the best candidate. All of the applicants had been asked to teach a lesson and Cindy had given one of the best lessons he had ever witnessed. On the other hand, Betty's presentation had included passing out commercially prepared worksheets to the class.

Although he did not observe the sample lessons, John agreed with the principal that Cindy was the obvious choice for the job. As one of the first tests of the new superintendent's site-based management plan, this situation was quite sensitive. Jim's explanation for what was happening was that the fourth grade teachers were intimidated by the excellence that Cindy would bring to the team and the school. They were much more comfortable with a candidate they knew and liked. By putting Cindy fourth on their list, they had made it extremely difficult for the assistant superintendent to recommend her to the superintendent.

John thought about meeting with the team and sharing what he had learned about all of the candidates from his telephone calls. At the same time, he questioned whether it was appropriate to talk with them about the "average" recommendations that had been given to their friend. If he forced the principal to accept Betty on his faculty, he would undoubtedly appear to be weak and less than supportive of the person most responsible for the school. On the other hand, overriding the recommendation of the fourth grade team might well be seen as a setback for the new superintendent's policy of collaboration with the teachers. He also thought about a possible compromise, the person who was number two on the teachers' list was in his mind a better choice than Betty. He knew that the next board meeting was only a week away and that he had to make his recommendations to the superintendent within the next two days.

## DISCUSSION QUESTIONS

1. Do you agree with the practice of allowing teacher committees to participate in the hiring process?

2. If you agree with the process, what would be the ideal system for such involvement?
3. What should John Stacy do about his recommendation on this position?


## ADDITIONAL RESOURCES

Briggs, Kerry L., and Priscilla Wholstetter. 1999. *Key Elements of a Successful School-Based Management Strategy*. February 7, 2007. http://www.ecs.org/html/off site.asp?document=http%3A%2F%2Fwww%2Eusc%2Eedu%2Fdept%2Feducation %2Fcegov%2Fpublications%2Fbriggsandwohlstetter1999%2Epdf.

*Critical Issue: Transferring Decision Making to Local Schools: Site-Based Management*. 1995. February 7, 2007. http://www.ncrel.org/sdrs/areas/issues/envrnmnt/go/ go100.htm.

De Grauwe, Anton. 2005. "Improving the Quality of Education through School-Based Management: Learning from International Experiences." *International Review of Education* 51 (4): 269–287.

Hansen, Janet S., Marguerite Roza 2005. "Decentralized Decision Making for Schools: New Promise for an Old Idea?" *Rand Education Occasional Paper*. February 7, 2007. http://www.rand.org/pubs/occasional_papers/2005/RAND_OP153.pdf.

Hill, Marie S., and DiAnn Casteel. "Perceptions of Responsibility for Decision Making: Hiring a Teacher." Paper presented at the Annual Meeting of the Mid-South Educational Regional Association, Nashville, TN, November 1994. February 7, 2007. http://www.eric.ed.gov/ERICDocs/data/ericdocs2/content_storage_01/0000000b/ 80/24/35/0a.pdf.

Holloway, John H. 2000. "The Promise and Pitfalls of Site-Based Management: How Does This Concept Work?" *Educational Leadership* 57(7). Retrieved February 7, 2007, from http://www.nea.org/teachexperience/chgk040627.html.

Van Allan S. 1991. "At Least Listen to the Principal." *Executive Educator* 13(4): 21–23.

# There is Just Not Enough Time in the School Day

## *school-sponsored activities*

**Schools in the United States have historically allowed numerous interruptions in the regular class schedule. Some of the activities that take away instructional time are school assemblies, academic and athletic trips, music lessons, and pull-out programs for remediation for special education students. We have also reduced the time students spend in class by adding an ever increasing number of tests. There is also a tendency to give at least half days for parent–teacher conferences and to allot a number of days each year for teacher conferences or in-service training. In comparison with other countries, students in the United States have fewer days of instruction and often shorter school days. Coupled with the fact that students on average spend less time with homework, it might well be concluded that these factors contribute heavily to the low ranking of our students in international test score comparisons.**

Terry Edwards had been a principal for ten years, and she could remember many conversations and arguments over various interruptions in the instructional day. Never before had she encountered such vehemence among faculty members in her middle school concerning this issue. During a recent meeting of the department chairpersons in her building, this problem came to the forefront. She decided to put the sixteen field trip requests that had been submitted for the coming year on the agenda. Faculty members had been asked to complete a form describing the field trip that they wished to take with their students. Among those submitted were requests for visits to museums, attendance at concerts, a lunch at a French restaurant, trips to the state park by science classes, and an overnight visit to the state capital.

Terry hoped that the input of her chairpersons would help her in deciding on the field trip requests. Instead, the issue had provoked a rather extended and heated debate. Without truly addressing the issue of the field trips, members of the group used the occasion to raise their personal concerns about interruptions of their classes.

The first one that came up was the Annual Career Day. For several years, the middle school guidance department had invited to the school parents and other community members to talk to interested students about their jobs or professions. Although policemen and undertakers often drew the biggest crowd, students signed up to hear about employment in such areas as nursing, teaching, and social work. The leader of the math department expressed his personal feeling that such a program would be more useful at the high school level rather than having it for twelve-, thirteen-, and fourteen-year-olds. Not everyone agreed with him, but it seemed that each member of the group had his or her own individual concern about interruptions during the school day.

Even though Terry had reduced the number of school assemblies, there were still five or six times a year when the entire student body was called to the auditorium for a speaker, a concert, or perhaps a short play. For instance, Terry remembered that during the previous semester there had been a speaker on the dangers of drug abuse and a holiday concert featuring the middle school chorus and band. During the second semester, along with the Career Day, there would be an academic recognition assembly, as well as a spelling bee and another guest speaker. Bob Grasso, the science chairperson, questioned the value of several of these assemblies and suggested that by eliminating them the school could gain some instructional time.

The issue that caused the greatest conflict during the meeting arose when someone questioned allowing students to miss class for music lessons or sectional rehearsals. Despite the fact that most of the school musicians were conscientious students who did well in their classes, the practice of allowing them to miss a class every six weeks was considered to have a negative effect on their work in the class by many of those at the meeting.

Steven Norman, the music chairperson, quickly and somewhat angrily pointed out that eliminating these lessons would ruin the school's instrumental program. He pointed out that the vast majority of the school's instrumental students could not afford private lessons and to do away with the music release time would be a disaster. Defending his program, he argued that the school band was a source of pride not only for the school but within the community. He referred to a thank-you note that the middle school band director had recently received from the American Legion. The letter had been very complimentary about the band's recent appearance at the Veteran's Day parade. Another person at the meeting suggested that perhaps the students could have less frequent lessons, but Steven claimed that anything less than the status quo would be unacceptable.

Phyllis Lambert, the chairperson of the English department had her own complaint. She was distressed by the number of times special education students were taken out of her classes. Even though she supported the inclusion movement and did not disagree that most special education students belonged in regular classes, she was upset by the amount of time some of these students spent outside of her sixth grade classroom for special services required in their Individualized Education Plans. She pointed to one student who was getting speech therapy, occupational therapy, and personal counseling. All of these pull-out services seemed to come during her language arts class. No one disagreed with the fact that this was a problem but there seemed to be no possible solution.

Of all the concerns expressed at the meeting, the one that all of the teachers agreed on was the amount of time now required for preparing for and administering mandated tests. Prior to the passage of the No Child Left Behind Act, the school had its own testing program, but the new mandates required additional yearly "high-stakes testing" in language arts, math, and science. Not only did these tests take away instructional time, but the amount of class time being devoted to teaching test-taking skills and in reviewing for the test, increased every year.

Summing up the many issues raised during the discussion, Bob observed that, "we are supposed to be raising our test scores, but it seems that we have less and less time for actual instruction." Near the end of the meeting, the discussion veered into even more sensitive areas when the English, math, and science chairpersons agreed that what they needed most to improve their students test scores was additional instructional time. They pointed out that the state had approved of some experimental new middle school schedules which reduced the time that students spent in art, music, and shop classes to gain more time for the "basic" subjects. Just bringing up this possibility had raised the stress level in the meeting, and Terry concluded that it might be best just to change the subject. She did not return to the issue of field trips, which had started the argument, concluding that probably each of the chairs would defend the application of their department members.

Terry now knew that many of the issues raised at this meeting would be ones that would continue as the pressures to provide additional instructional time would not be lessening. At the end of the session, she suggested, without thinking, that all of these problems could be solved if they could just add fifteen days to the school year. Bob quickly responded to this solution by telling her to "go talk to the union."

As she packed her briefcase to leave for home after what seemed like a very long day, Terry looked out the window and noticed that snow was beginning to fall. She couldn't help but think that weather might be yet another reason for losing instructional time but she secretly knew that she was more than ready for a snow day.

## DISCUSSION QUESTIONS

1. Are field trips useful educational experiences? If a school is going to sponsor field trips, what factors should be considered in approving them?
2. Are school assemblies a valid school activity? What are some examples of assemblies which might be justifiable interruptions of the school day?
3. Do you support releasing students from class for music lessons? If such a practice is allowed, what policy should be used to govern this release time?
4. How can a school minimize the interruptions caused by the necessity of providing mandated services for special education students?
5. Would you support allowing middle schools to rearrange their schedules to provide more instructional time for language arts, math, and science, even if it meant reducing time for other subjects? If so, what subjects might be given less time?
6. What, if anything, should Terry Edwards do about the discussion that took place during the meeting of the department chairs?

## ADDITIONAL RESOURCES

Elovitz, Leonard H. 2002. "Let's Cut Out All These Classroom Interruptions." *Principal* 8(5): 57–58. Hong, Laraine K. 2001. "Too Many Intrusions on Instructional Time." *Phi Delta Kappan* 89 (9):712–714. Leonard, Lawrence J. 2001. "Erosion of Instructional Time: Teacher Concerns." Paper presented at the Annual Meeting of the Mid-South Educational Research Association, Little Rock, AR, November 2001. February 7, 2007. http://www.eric.ed.gov/ERICDocs/data/ericdocs2/content_storage_01/0000000b/80/0d/a7/34.pdf.

Leonard, Leonard J. 2001. "From Indignation to Indifference: Teacher Concerns about Externally Imposed Classroom Interruptions." *Journal of Educational Research* 95: 103–109. Queen, J. Allen, and Patsy S. Queen. 2004. *The Frazzled Teacher's Wellness Plan: A Five Step Program for Reclaiming Time, Managing Stress, and Creating a Healthy Lifestyle.* London: Sage.

# The Strike

## *unions*

**Strikes by teachers and other school personnel are legal in many states. Even where they are not lawful, they occur when a union feels that all of the other alternatives have been exhausted. The failure to report to work becomes a final tactic used by unions in what is usually a prolonged effort to arrive at a contract settlement with their school districts. Strikes or even the threat of a strike can create high levels of stress in any school. As a middle manager the school principal is frequently in a very uncomfortable position as he or she attempts to maintain a positive relationship with the strikers as well as with the central administration and the board of education. The situation is complicated by the fact that in many areas of the country, principals have organized units that negotiate terms and conditions of employment with their school district. Sometimes it is quite difficult for a school principal not to be sympathetic with the unhappy employees especially when they also may feel poorly treated by the district themselves.**

All of the nonteaching personnel in the Ridgemont Central School District had been on strike for three days. Although the district's teachers were working, most of them felt great empathy for the staff members who were on strike. In fact, Marjorie Schultz, the principal of the Ridgemont Elementary School, noticed when she entered and left school the past three days that several teachers had joined the picket line. Last evening at the elementary school's winter concert at least twenty-five of her teaching staff had joined the teacher aides, administrative assistants, cafeteria workers, and even the school nurse as they demonstrated in front of the school.

As parents and grandparents entered the concert, strikers were engaged in some rather heated discussions. It seemed clear that many of those forced to walk through the pickets on both sides of the sidewalk were not happy with the strikers. Although there were no major incidents, there was heightened tension in the district. Driving home from the concert Marjorie couldn't help but think if the strike continued there might be bigger problems.

Although she was able to have several friendly conversations with the picketers when she entered and left the building, the lack of progress in settling the dispute was making everyone in the school uneasy. Despite the growing tension, the board of education was determined to keep the school open. Because of the board's conviction that money was not available to raise salaries beyond the offer that had already been given to the union, there seemed to be no way to break the impasse without raising property taxes in the district. The majority of the board members were convinced that the community would be very unhappy with any tax increase. The fact that the school district had an 8 percent unemployment rate and had suffered the loss of several major businesses led some citizens to call for a reduction in the tax rate. Two of the newly elected board members had included a promise to seek a reduction in the property tax in their campaign literature.

On the other hand, both the teachers and the nonteaching personnel were receiving salaries that were lower than most of the neighboring districts. To make matters worse, the board insisted that all employees pay a larger percentage of the cost of their health insurance. With these outstanding issues, it was hard for anyone to see the possibility of a quick settlement. Adding to the problem was the fact that the contract between the teacher union and the school district would end in three months. Negotiations had already begun, and the teachers had been given a report from the union leadership that there had been no progress in reaching a settlement.

For Marjorie, the three days of the strike had been exhausting. She was answering the phone, doing her own typing and filing, and had been forced to assist some parent volunteers in emptying the garbage from the cafeteria. Because the nurse was also honoring the strike, she was constantly running to the nurse's office to help the substitute nurse who was distributing medicine and dealing with children who were, or at least said they were, sick. In one case, she was forced to call a physician to clarify the instructions for administering a student's medicine.

Although Marjorie knew she could endure the current situation, she was beginning to have trouble dealing with her administrative colleagues as well as the teachers in her building. As the senior principal in the district, she was receiving calls from other principals who were experiencing hostility from their employees. One principal was in tears on the phone and suggested that the administrative group meet and go en masse to inform the superintendent that the conditions in all of their schools had become intolerable. Although she was sympathetic with her colleague, she was not ready to complain. If she was concerned about her fellow administrators, she was even more worried about her relationship with the staff and the teachers in her building.

Of all the strikers, Marjorie was most troubled about her relationship with her personal administrative assistant, Gwen Kay, who had voted against the strike but could not bring herself to abandon her friends in the nonteaching bargaining unit. When Gwen asked her how things were going the evening outside the auditorium, Majorie wasn't sure how to answer. All that she could think to say was, "Gwen, I can't wait until you come back to work. I have never appreciated you more than during these last three days." Having answered this way, she was not sure whether she had made Gwen feel better or worse.

Increasingly Marjorie was becoming uneasy with how the teachers were dealing with the strike. One day in the cafeteria Mary Lyon, a third grade teacher, noticed Marjorie carrying out a garbage bag. Mary said to her, "it appears that you are aiding and abetting the enemy." If this was meant as a joke, it had been delivered with a level of intensity that signified that Mary did not approve of the principal doing the work of the striking cafeteria workers. There were other indications that the teachers thought that she had become a lackey of the board. When another teacher saw her working in the health office, she questioned Marjorie about her competence in doing the work of a nurse.

As if all of this was not bad enough, all of the principals received a memo from the central office ordering them to begin to talk with substitute teachers about whether they would be willing to work in the schools if there was a teacher strike. If such a strike were to occur, the principals were authorized to offer the substitutes $250 a day for their work. These conversations were to be held confidentially, but Marjorie was quite certain that even one such conversation would quickly be reported to members of the faculty. Once again, the principals would be in a very awkward position with the teachers in their building who had yet to even have formal discussions about a possible strike.

Tomorrow the strike would enter its fourth day with no end in sight. Marjorie hated the position she was in as a middle manager trying to keep the school functioning without endangering her relationship with the central administration, the staff, or the faculty. Still, she saw no alternative but to try to persevere.

## DISCUSSION QUESTIONS

1. Do you support the right of school personnel to strike? Why? Why not?
2. In the case of a strike or any job actions, what is the primary role of the principal? Is this role any different than that of the superintendent?

3. What, if anything, can Marjorie do to get through the crisis caused by the strike?

## ADDITIONAL RESOURCES

Black, Susan. 2002. "Reforming the Unions: Does the 'New Unionism' Pay Off in Student Achievement? The Jury's Still Out." *American School Board Journal* 189(2): 44–47.

Francis, Lorie, James E. Cameron, and E. Kevin Kelloway. "Crossing the Line: Violence on the Picket Line." In *Handbook of Workplace Violence*, edited by E. Kevin Kelloway, Julian Barling, and J. Joseph Hurrell, 231–260. Thousand Oaks, CA: Sage.

Jazzar, Michael. 2006. "Leading a Unionized Elementary School." *NAESP: National Association of Elementary School Principals.* February 2, 2007. http://www.naesp.org/ContentLoad.do?contentID=1860. (Reprinted from *Principal* 85(4): 70)

*Case Study 5*

# The Wild Coach

*personnel problems*

**A major function of school district athletic directors is to hire and supervise all of the coaches of the interscholastic sports teams. Often it is a challenging task to find and keep competent individuals in these positions. Coaching, especially at the high school level, requires a great deal of time and can also be a source of stress to both the coaches and the athletic director. High school teams are of great interest not only to the student body but often to the entire community. Teachers, of all those who might consider a coaching position, find that the long practices, frequent trips, and evening games can negatively affect their regular classroom responsibilities. This is especially true if the teacher has family responsibilities. As a result, athletic directors must attempt to be as supportive as possible to those teachers who are willing to take on the heavy responsibility of coaching. At the same time, like any administrator, an athletic director must at times deal with sensitive personnel problems. This responsibility can be especially challenging if the coach involved is working in a sport that has a high degree of community visibility.**

Fred Ross had been the athletic director at Madison High School for twenty-two years and during that time, he had faced a number of difficult situations. Known for his quiet diplomacy, Coach Ross had become something of a father figure for the physical education department as well as for all of the district's coaches. As the high school tennis coach, he had also built a very strong program that had achieved several league championships. A significant group of his tennis players had gone on to become state champions in their classification. Fred thought of a coach as primarily a teacher, and he almost never used the emotional pep talks, which are a part of the repertoire of many coaches. Preferring to stay in the background during tennis matches, he was most concerned with helping students not only become better tennis players, but more important for him, guiding them in becoming better people.

In addition, he was vehement in insisting that his athletes take their school work seriously. Fred communicated frequently with the teachers of his team members to ensure that the athletes on his team were keeping up with their school work. During his career as an athletic director and a coach, he had tried in his own way to model these concerns for all of the coaches in the district.

It was obvious that the current varsity basketball coach, Mike Kendall, had not fully accepted Fred's approach to coaching. Mike was in his fourth year as a popular social studies teacher in the high school. Following the completion of his third year, he had gained tenure and even with his heavy responsibility as a coach, he had the reputation of being a popular and effective classroom teacher.

A college basketball player, Mike had been the junior varsity coach for two years before being promoted to the varsity job. Even as a JV coach, he had outbursts that had caused him to be given technical fouls by the referee. Fred had talked to Mike several times about the fact that part of a coach's role was to teach his students good sportsmanship. Mike had quietly accepted the advice and by the end of the second year as a JV coach, he appeared to have developed more self-control. At the time he was appointed as the varsity coach, Fred had again emphasized the importance of setting a good example, especially during a game when the gym was packed with students, parents, and community members.

During his initial year as the varsity basketball coach, Mike had received six technical fouls during the eighteen-game season. As a spectator at most of the games, Fred thought that his coach was becoming increasingly excitable as the season progressed. Mike seldom sat down during a game, and he constantly argued with officials as they ran by the Madison bench. Several times he had raised his arms in the air and shouted so that he could be heard even in the noisy gym. Although the team did not win the league championship his first year, they won twelve of their games, and most of the key players were returning for Mike's second year as the head coach. In his evaluation conference following the last game, Fred praised him for his commitment and enthusiasm but was critical of his behavior during games and of the many technical fouls that his actions had caused.

Expectations for Mike's second year as the varsity coach were very high as four of the five starters were experienced seniors. Beginning with the first home game, the gym was often full even before the JV games began, and as the season progressed the community's interest in the team increased along with the expectation of a possible league championship. After winning the first five games, the team went into a slump and lost two close contests to schools they were expected to beat. Up until that point, Mike had only had one technical foul. In the eighth game, he had an explosion when the referee called a fifth foul on the team's star point guard. After arguing with the referee, he threw a towel onto the floor and received a technical foul and a warning from the official.

The day after that episode, Fred called him into his office for a conference. For the first time, Mike attempted to defend his behavior. He claimed that talking with the referees during the game, "helped keep them on their toes," and would help "make them think twice about calling fouls on his team." In addition, he claimed that he was always in control of himself during games and that at times he staged his tirades not only to motivate his team but also to "get the crowd into the game." He believed that the local fans enjoyed his "little displays" and as a result they too would "get on the refs." It was his belief that his behavior stimulated the intensity of his team and excited the crowd.

It was evident to Fred that his coach believed in what he was doing as he suggested that he was doing what all of the great college and professional coaches did when he "jawboned" the referees. As far as his team was concerned, "they get a kick out of it when I carry on with the refs." At this meeting Fred's sermon about coaches being first and foremost teachers and role models seemed to have no influence on the basketball coach.

As Fred thought about the meeting, he was alarmed by Mike's attitude, and he asked that the high school principal, Heather Chan, talk to the coach. Heather was a former music teacher who was very interested in the school's academic program but did not often become involved in athletics. Out of duty, she attended one contest of every sports team each year. The evening she chose to go to one of the boy's basketball games, Mike was on his good behavior. Heather spoke with Mike but their talk had little impact. By the fifteenth game of the season, Mike already had seven technical fouls. It was during game sixteen that the issue became critical. Late in the game, Madison was behind by five points to a team that had won only a few games. With three minutes to go, when one of the referees felt that he had taken enough criticism from Mike, he called a technical foul on the coach.

This time, Mike did not control himself, and one minute after the first technical was called he screamed at the same referee again and slammed his clipboard on the bench. The referee stopped the game and not only called a second technical foul but ordered the coach to leave the gym. At that point Mike had to be restrained by his assistant coach who eventually was able to escort him to the locker room. During his exit from the gym, some in the crowd cheered for their angry coach who was still yelling at the referee. The cheering was mixed with some booing, which seemed to come primarily from the fans supporting the visiting team. Ironically, following the incident the Madison boys rallied and came back to win the game.

Fred knew that his basketball coach had many supporters in the community and even among the faculty. At the same time, he heard from many regular fans and teachers that they were ashamed of the coach's behavior. There was little question that most, if not all of the players, would support the coach if the school attempted any disciplinary action. Immediately following the game, Fred was ready to go into the locker room and fire his coach. He decided instead to give himself the weekend to calm down and to think about the issue more before making a decision.

On Sunday evening, he decided to call Heather to get her input. During the conversation the athletic director explained that if the team won the next two games Madison High School would earn its first league basketball championship in twenty-one years. He also pointed out that the local newspaper and many alumni would be watching the school closely to see how the authorities reacted to the coach's behavior. Hearing all of this, Heather said that she wanted to talk to the superintendent. Later that evening Fred received a call from the superintendent who, after hearing the whole story, agreed to support the athletic director in a disciplinary action. Asked if this support included firing the coach, the superintendent, after a long pause, said, "Yes, it's your call."

As Fred tossed and turned in bed that evening, he thought of three possible courses of action.

1. He could fire the coach and appoint one of his assistants for the remainder of the year.
2. He could suspend the coach for one or more games.
3. He could write a stern final warning and place it in the coach's personnel file.

Whatever he was going to do, it should happen that Monday afternoon.

## DISCUSSION QUESTIONS

1. List what, for you, should be the three most important goals of a school's interscholastic sports program. Place these three goals in the order of priority for you.
2. Should a team's winning percentage be a factor in evaluating the work of a coach?
3. If you were responsible for establishing a formal evaluation procedure for coaches, how would you do it?
4. In interviewing candidates for coaching positions, what are three questions you would ask during the interview?
5. What should Fred do about his basketball coach?

## ADDITIONAL RESOURCES

Bennett, Lisa. 1998. "New Game Plan: Coaches Tackle the Issues of Violence and Disrespect in Sports." *Teaching Tolerance* 7(2): 21–27.

Jones, Dianne C. 2004. "Domain 1: Philosophy and Ethics National Standards for Sport Coaches." *Strategies: A Journal for Physical and Sport Educators* 17(4): 23–24.

Jordan, Jeremy S., T. Christopher Greenwell, Alan L. Geist, Donna L. Pastore, and Daniel F. Mahony. 2004. "Coaches' Perceptions of Conference Code of Ethics." *Physical Educator* 61: 131–145.

Myers, Nicholas D., Deborah L. Feltz, Kimberly S. Maier, Edward W. Wolfe, and Mark D. Reckase. 2006. "Athletes' Evaluations of Their Head Coach's Coaching Competency." *Research Quarterly for Exercise and Sport* 77: 111–121.

Wiersma, Lenny D., and Clay P. Sherman. 2005. "Volunteer Youth Sport Coaches' Perspectives of Coaching Education/Certification and Parental Codes of Conduct." *Research Quarterly for Exercise and Sport* 76: 324–339.

# How Do We Improve Reading Scores?

## *curriculum development*

**The No Child Left Behind legislation, signed by President Bush in 2002, has affected every public school in America. It certainly has had a major impact on the job of every building principal. In the past, it was possible for a person to be a successful principal if he or she could maintain a well-disciplined school environment and not alienate students, faculty, parents, the superintendent of schools, or the board of education. With the introduction of the mandatory high-stakes test and the school accountability measures built into the law, principals now must become what is being called "an instructional leader." Even if an individual performs well in the traditional roles of a principal, if the test scores in the school decline over two or more years, the administrator could be in trouble. Unfortunately, many school administrators are not well prepared to lead an initiative designed to raise the test scores of their students. This case study deals with such a challenge.**

David Edwin was sitting in his office reflecting on the meeting of third grade teachers that he had just left. He was more worried now than at any time during his almost ten months as the administrator of the Riverside Elementary School. As a result of the session, he knew he was facing a major challenge. Having begun his first administrative position just one week after his thirty-fifth birthday, he was feeling ill-prepared and inadequate as he sought to develop a plan for dealing with the problems faced by his school. On the other hand, he was aware that he possessed some advantages that other first-year principals could not call upon. Because he had spent a full semester as an administrative intern at the school the previous year, he did have some knowledge concerning the faculty and staff and also about the school program.

When he began his assignment as an intern of the principal, Linda Bourges, who was planning to retire at the end of the year, he never considered the possibility that he would be her replacement. With Linda's blessing and the support of a significant number of the faculty, he was selected from a field of candidates, many of whom had more experience than he did. During his eight years as a sixth grade teacher in one of the other elementary schools in the city, he had the opportunity to serve as the grade-level chairperson for four years. In addition, he was a member of a number of faculty committees. On several of these he acted as chairperson. His placement file contained numerous positive references from his former administrators and college professors. Finally, he had demonstrated his leadership ability in the community as an active member of the Rotary Club and the Public Library Board. On the negative side, David was aware that unlike many first-year principals, he never had served as an assistant principal.

Even with this lack of experience, his first year had gone very well and for the most part he was feeling comfortable in his new position. His comfort level had suffered a major blow the previous week when the school district received the results of the state language arts test. This examination was a requirement in grades three through eight as part of the No Child Left Behind Act. After studying the results, David realized that they could not have been much worse for his school. In the city district where Riverside Elementary was located, his overall student scores placed the school in sixth place among the seven elementary schools. Within the county, the outcome was even worse. All of the suburban and rural schools had higher scores. Adding to the dilemma was the fact that this was the second year in a row that the overall scores had declined. There was no question in David's mind that he would need to quickly develop a language arts improvement plan.

After the initial panic caused by the results, he decided it would be a mistake to overreact. One possibility was to confer with Dr. Catherina Schrieber, the assistant superintendent for instruction. He knew that as an instructional expert she was very knowledgeable, but he really wanted to work with his own faculty to develop an improvement plan. He was somewhat afraid of being pushed by an expert into an initiative that would be resisted by his teachers. With this in mind, he scheduled separate grade level meetings for those teachers assigned at the levels where the exams were given. Following these sessions, he planned also to meet with the kindergarten, first, and second grade teams. David chose to begin with the third grade for several reasons. It was at this grade level where students began to take the mandatory tests, and it was also the grade level with the lowest scores. In addition it occurred to him that this team might be the most difficult one to engage. Now that he had had a meeting with them, he was sure that it was going to be a major challenge to develop a consensus surrounding any improvement plan.

Because he had spent a semester at the school as an intern, David knew something about each of the third grade teachers. The senior member of the team, Margaret Burns, had already passed her sixtieth birthday and was probably just a year or two from retirement. She was considered by almost everybody who knew her as an "old fashioned teacher," who could easily pose for a picture as a typical grandmother. In fact, she had seven grandchildren who ranged in ages from three to thirteen. In terms of her approach to teaching reading, David knew that she relied almost exclusively on the district's basal reading program, which had been adopted by the district several years ago. Unlike many teachers, she taught her lessons using the exact wording in the teacher's manual. She believed heavily in the use of phonics and also had her students use a separate spelling series as well as a workbook published by the same company as the reading books. Although she had been exposed to several whole language workshops, she never really accepted any part of this approach. In fact, in a conversation last year she mentioned to David her opinion that whole language was a "failed experiment."

Her younger colleague, Jennifer Klein, had been trained extensively in the whole language method and a visit to her classroom quickly made it evident that she was committed to both the theory and practice of this approach. Although at times she used the stories in the district's reading series, Jennifer often substituted what she believed was the best children's literature. In doing so she would frequently use "big books" to help stimulate involvement and interest in the stories. Instead of using separate spelling and grammar workbooks, she chose her spelling lessons from the books that her students were reading. Although it was not ignored in her classroom, phonics was not emphasized. Instead she spent time teaching students to use context clues to identify unfamiliar words. Perhaps the most obvious feature in her classroom was the extensive library she had accumulated over the years. It was secretly envied by every other teacher in the building even though some teachers may have resented the fact that she had been able to personally purchase almost all of the books.

The fact that Jennifer's husband was a successful physician in the city allowed her to buy whatever she wished. This included a personal wardrobe which was considerably more stylish than any other individual working in the school. Despite the fact that she was in her mid-forties, Jennifer looked every bit the young professional woman, even on "Dress Down Fridays" when she wore expensive designer clothing. Active politically in the city, she had been the chairperson of the city Democratic Party for a time. With her bachelor's degree from Vassar and a master's from Teachers College at Columbia, Jennifer was at home with the intellectual elite in the city, and at the same time she also was close to a select group of the Riverside faculty.

David's thoughts now turned to a third member of the team whom he thought of as a typical "soccer mom." In her mid-thirties, Heather DeLevin had three children all younger than age twelve and spent many evenings at either soccer or little league baseball games. Transporting the children was primarily her responsibility as her husband was a deputy sheriff who frequently worked the night shift. David had noticed that Heather sometimes looked and acted very tired. During the eleven years of her teaching career, she had taken three maternity leaves and also had been forced to take a significant number of days off for sickness and family reasons. Even though she was a hardworking teacher, she still spent less time on her job than the other members of her team. Philosophically and in terms of teaching techniques, she seemed to fall somewhere between her two older colleagues.

The newest member of the team was currently in her second year of teaching. A graduate with both a bachelor's and master's degree from a local Methodist college, Rebecca Taylor had learned about the recent theories and methods being used in language arts. Yet as a twenty-four-year-old new teacher, she was somewhat reserved during faculty meetings. Naturally quiet and somewhat shy, Rebecca made a conscious effort to fit into the third grade team and avoided any arguments that occurred during the meetings

Thinking back on how the meeting had begun, David remembered that immediately following his introductory remarks, Margaret had jumped right into the discussion. Going on the offensive, she pointed out that in recent years far too many third grade children were not ready for third grade work. Many of them were reading below the second grade level when they came to the third grade. She went on to say that, "We are not miracle workers. I remember when I first started teaching here, they used to retain those kids who were not making it in the first or second grade." She went on to recall that it was not unusual to hold back ten or more students in the second grade. Margaret believed that, "had we done that last year, our third grade reading scores would have been more acceptable."

Glancing at the other three teachers in the room, David did not observe that there was a great deal of enthusiasm for this solution. He also questioned whether the retention of more first and second graders would solve the problem. Margaret was not through sharing her ideas and with her next observation it was hard to disagree. She pointed out that the children attending Riverside Elementary School had changed during her career. There were more Hispanic students, many of whom were still learning the English language. In addition, there were numerous special education students who had been taken out of self-contained classrooms and placed in the regular third grade classes. Although no one disagreed with this fact, someone had pointed out that the same thing was happening in other neighborhood schools in the city.

Next to offer a plan had been Jennifer, who explained in detail a plan that was new to everyone in the room. Called "Positive Deviancy," it was an approach being used to bring about change at the local hospital. As David understood the process, a pair of individuals from Tufts University helped the employees of the hospital to identify their problems and then assisted them in finding similar hospitals that were dealing effectively with those problems and to implement some of the successful methods being used at the facilities they had visited. Jen said that this couple from Tufts had also used the same technique with schools as they were using in the local hospital.

Having picked up on the possibility of travel, Margaret suggested that, "they might visit some schools in the south where it was warmer. If that doesn't work, how about Las Vegas?" Allowing himself a brief smile, David went on to raise a number of questions about the "Positive Deviancy." No one else in the group appeared to be overly interested.

At that point, Heather entered the discussion. She recalled that in her first year at Riverside, the faculty had engaged in an extensive process that ended in the adoption of the reading series that they had been using for the past ten years. She remembered sitting in meetings, listening to company representatives explain the virtues of their books. In conversations with teachers from other schools in the city, she had learned that no other school was using the reading series they were using at Riverside. It was her thought that perhaps they had fallen behind. She argued for a new round of discussions with publishers as a good way to, "find out what is out there." Finally, she observed that such a process "might also bring us together in that presently, we all seem to be doing our own thing."

After David had encouraged her to share her thoughts, Rebecca spoke up. As the only member of the team with a master's degree in literacy, she seemed to speak with authority about what was going on in the field. She concluded with the suggestion that the school invite Naomi Garwood, a reading professor from her college, to come and work with the entire faculty. She explained that Professor Garwood was extremely knowledgeable about teaching reading and that everyone would love working with her.

Margaret obviously seemed to doubt the wisdom of calling on a college education professor. She recalled that she never learned a thing in any of her education classes, pointing out that she doubted that "any of my professors had ever spent very much time in a real elementary classroom." Jennifer observed that she had encountered several brilliant education professors, especially at Columbia.

Looking at the clock, David had noticed that it was almost 4:30 p.m., and he had felt at the time that everyone had at least had had an opportunity to be heard. In closing the meeting, he thanked the team for their "valuable suggestions" and explained to them that he would prepare some minutes of the meeting to share with them. He also let them know that after he had met with all of the grade level teams, he would then work with the entire faculty to prepare a plan for raising the language arts scores. Heather got the last word in when she asked, "what are we going to do if the math and science test scores are as bad as those in reading?" David shuttered as he thought about this sobering possibility. All that he could think to say was, "we will face that if it happens, meanwhile, thank you for your work today."

Thinking about the variety of possible plans that could be adopted, David decided to stop at a college library on his way home and to take out some books on teaching children to read. He knew that he had a lot to learn.

## DISCUSSION QUESTIONS

1. Did David make a mistake in not first consulting with the assistant superintendent for instruction?
2. Were these initial grade level meetings a good way to begin to create a plan for improving the reading scores?
3. How did you react to the various suggestions made at the meeting?
   a. Additional retention of students before they reach third grade
   b. Exploring the concept of "Positive Deviancy"
   c. Seeking to select a new reading series for the school
   d. Bringing in a consultant from a local college to work with the faculty
4. What other courses of action might David consider in developing a language arts improvement plan?

## ADDITIONAL RESOURCES

Black, Susan. 2007. What's Being Said about NCLB? *American School Board Journal* 194(5): 41–43.

Cawelti, Gordon. 2006. "The Side Effects of NCLB." *Educational Leadership* 64(3): 64–68.

Reese, William J. 2005. *America's Public Schools: From the Common School to "No Child Left Behind."* Baltimore: Johns Hopkins University Press.

Toch, Thomas. 2006. "Turmoil in the Testing Industry." *Educational Leadership* 64(3): 53–57.

Vu, Pauline. 2007. Lake Wobegon, U.S.A.—Where All the Children are above Average. *Stateline.org*. February 2, 2007. http://www.stateline.org/live/deatils/story?contentID=172668.

## Case Study 7

# The Mothers for Decent Lunches

## *health concerns*

**Concerns about the increasing number of American students classified as obese is one of several factors that has prompted critics to question the lunches being served in our schools. Specifically people have been troubled by the amount of sugar and fat that students are consuming in school cafeterias. Others point to the failure of school lunches to provide appetizing, nutritional options that could help our nation's children to develop healthy eating habits. Districts throughout the country have experienced efforts by concerned adults to alter their school's food service program.**

Assistant Superintendent for Business Richard Lopez had a problem that was being complicated by what was, at least at the moment, a small community uprising. Although he had experienced controversial issues dealing with the district's transportation, maintenance, and office personnel, he had never been particularly concerned about the cafeteria program. The fact was that this department had run quite smoothly during his five years of managing the nonteaching staff in his school district. He felt quite fortunate that the various nonteaching groups had united into a single union after a long period during which each of them had their own organization. This split had made it necessary for him to negotiate four separate contracts. Still, a new union that was affiliated with a national union could be difficult. Fortunately, at least up until that point, the union was not involved with his current problem, but the way the situation was developing, it seemed quite likely that he would soon have the local representative of the national union in his office. This was not something he enjoyed.

The current crisis arose in the middle school with the formation of a group that called itself The Mothers for Decent Lunches. The women involved were concerned with the significant number of overweight children in the middle school. As the group attempted to determine the causes of this problem, they decided that a major focus should be to ensure that the students in the Middletown Middle School were eating well-balanced lunches that would reduce their caloric intake.

After their first meeting, a petition was circulated in the community calling for the elimination of the current a la carte option in the lunch program. Their primary focus was getting rid of the ability of students to eat pizza, hamburgers, hot dogs, and french fries everyday. Even though they could order a salad or a different nutritional lunch, few children chose to do so.

Gertrude Stern was the supervisor of the middle school cafeteria. She had held this position for twenty-three years. Earlier in her career she had been a leader in what was now remembered as the "Cafeteria War." Although he had not yet come to the Middletown District, Richard had heard about the issue, which had caused such a conflict in the district. At the time, the Middletown District Board of Education was facing severe budget difficulties and was searching for ways to reduce spending. One of the ways the board initially thought would be an effective economy measure was to contract out the food service program. Doing so would allow the district to no longer subsidize the cafeteria program. The previous school budget had authorized thirty-eight thousand dollars to help fund the school cafeterias in the district.

Gertrude had led the thirty-five district cafeteria workers in opposing this initiative. Given that all of the workers were district residents, cafeteria staff members had considerable community support in their effort to block the move to private contracting. After several months of petitions, picketing, and a letter-writing campaign to the local newspaper, a compromise was reached. The result was a decision that removed the budget subsidy but allowed the cafeteria staff to remain school district employees and administer the program. Although there had been periodic squabbles about bookkeeping issues, such as whether the food service program should pay for electricity or cleaning and maintaining the cafeteria, the arrangement seemed to be working.

Unfortunately, one of the byproducts of forcing the cafeteria program to at least break even had been the introduction of the a la carte menu. For a short time Gertrude had even been able to place soda machines in the middle school but a minor parent uprising brought this practice to an abrupt end. Even before the emergence of The Mothers for Decent Lunches, there was an underlying conflict occurring within the district's cafeteria program.

The previous year, the school board hired Victoria Green to be the director of the six school cafeterias in the district. She worked out of the central office and reported directly to Richard. A young woman with a bachelor's degree in nutrition from Cornell University, she came to her job with a clear vision of what a school cafeteria program should be. During her first year and a half in Middletown she had worked with the managers of the four elementary school cafeteria programs. She had some success in improving the nutritional value of meals at these schools. Victoria was currently also beginning to have discussions with the cafeteria manager at the high school. Richard had urged her several times to be as diplomatic as possible in trying to bring about any changes. Based on his advice, she had decided to save Gertrude until last, as they both agreed that she would be the least open to change. He was especially sensitive to Victoria's views about the middle school as she had already concluded that it would be possible to reduce the number of workers on the middle school cafeteria staff especially if the a la carte line was eliminated.

Despite their tacit agreement to not immediately stir up problems at the middle school, the previous week Victoria had decided to call upon Gertrude. The reason for her decision to have the conversation was that the middle school cafeteria was barely breaking even financially, and she felt it was her duty to talk directly to the person responsible for the program. The conversation had been a disaster as the two women were unable to agree on anything. The issue that caused Gertrude the most concern was when Victoria raised the idea of possibly cutting the a la carte line and reducing the number of cafeteria workers at the middle school.

To support her argument, Victoria pointed out that the middle school cafeteria staff was the largest in the district with eight employees working five hours a day. In comparison, the high school program, which served almost as many students, had only six individuals employed. It seemed to Victoria that the middle school program could survive even without the a la carte line if six workers could operate the program. She thought that Gertrude would be somewhat accepting because of the fact that the two middle school employees had seniority, they would replace two less senior workers in one of the elementary school cafeterias. This was true because all of the eight employees at the middle school had worked in the district for at least fifteen years. This had not given Gertrude any comfort, and she vehemently argued that all of the current staff was needed in the middle school.

When he heard about the conversation, Richard was not happy with his cafeteria director as he had not authorized her to talk about cutting positions. Victoria knew that the situation was not good at the middle school when she had visited there the day after the conversation with Gertrude. She was all but ignored by the cafeteria workers, and even the custodian who cleaned the lunch room would not speak to her. It was clear that her idea of cutting staff and taking away the food that the kids loved was already common knowledge. Most of the cafeteria staff supported the a la carte line as long as nutritious alternatives were available. They agreed with Gertrude that the students were old enough to decide on their own diet and even questioned why The Mothers for Decent Lunches didn't monitor the food choices of their own children.

Richard had not talked to the superintendent about this brewing problem but with the mothers' group planning to present their petition at the next board meeting, he knew that the superintendent would want to be informed. As he considered the various parties in the dispute, one major concern was Victoria's relationship with the cafeteria staff of the entire district. Of course as her superior, he could make a decision but at this point he had not yet decided what was best. He knew that the mothers would not give up their campaign easily, but if the a la carte line ceased to exist there could be financial problems if something else was not done. If they were to follow Victoria's inclination to cut two cafeteria workers, he was sure that he soon would be visited by a very upset union representative.

At this point Richard didn't know whether he would rather upset the mothers or the cafeteria staff. As he was considering his dilemma he remembered what a former superintendent and mentor had once said to him. Bill Lansing had told him on the day he retired from the district, "always ask yourself, what is best for the kids." He wasn't sure if this advice helped him with his problem, but he knew that he had to do something soon.

## DISCUSSION QUESTIONS

1. What are the advantages and disadvantages of school districts contracting out such services as the cafeteria program and district transportation?
2. Should school districts subsidize the school cafeteria program, or should they merely raise prices to ensure that any costs to the district are eliminated?
3. What would you suggest that Richard do to resolve his cafeteria crisis?

## ADDITIONAL RESOURCES

Lewis, Anne C. 2006. "Multi-Caused Obesity." *Education Digest: Essential Readings Condensed for Quick Review* 71(6): 70–71.

Meyer, M. K., Lambert, L., and Blackwell, A. 2002. "Choosing to Eat School Lunch: Child, Parent, or Joint Decision?" *Journal of Family & Consumer Sciences: From Research to Practice* 94(2): 24–28.

Vail, K. (2004). Raising the (salad) bar on obesity. *American School Board Journal* 191(1), 22–25. Retrieved April 21, 2007, from Academic Search Premier.

*Case Study 8*

# The Dilemma of Charter Schools

## *school choice*

School choice is an idea that has been with us since the middle of the twentieth century. The idea of establishing a school voucher program was first proposed by Milton Friedman in 1955. Although no voucher plan was introduced into the public school scene until late in the twentieth century, other forms of choice emerged as early as the 1960s. Magnet schools appeared in many large districts in part to offer parents and students a choice of public high schools. Examples might include a school for the arts, sciences, or one designed specifically for honors students. The purpose was to provide a special focus for the educational program. It was hoped that these options would also help to break down the neighborhood concept of schools which were tending to segregate students by race.

The charter school movement became popular beginning in the early 1990s. The theory behind charter schools was to allow interested individuals and groups to establish schools that, for the most part, were free of all local and state regulations. This freedom would allow experimentation that might also provide models that would improve all public schools. Because charter schools are public schools that are funded by state and local taxes, they have become a source of conflict at both the state and local levels.

Dr. Brandon Wernell, superintendent of the Riverdale City School District, knew he would be expected to comment on the resolution concerning charter schools which was to be debated at next week's school board meeting. The newest member of the board, Jessica King, had asked Brandon to place a motion on the agenda, calling for the board to draft a letter to its local state legislator supporting the governor's proposal to allow the doubling of the number of charter schools in the state.

For one of the first times in the state, city voters in Riverdale had elected to the board of education a parent of students who were enrolled in one of the local charter schools. Jessica had, for the past five years, been a champion of the charter school movement. As an African American parent, she felt that the city schools were not doing all that they might for minority children. At least in part, she had attributed the problem to a "bloated," "conservative," and "less than creative," school district bureaucracy. She also was very critical of the teacher union, which she believed only wanted to maintain status quo.

The aspirations for the supporters of charter schools had been given a boost when the newly elected governor included funds to double the number of charter schools in his proposed budget. In doing so, he had recommended that districts starting new charter schools be given additional state aid. This provision was meant to gain the support for charter schools of city districts that had been spending their own funds for those charter schools that were approved. The fact that Riverdale was one of the larger districts in the state, Brandon fully expected that there would be applications to begin additional schools in the city. Currently, there were three charter schools operating in Riverdale even though there had been serious reservations expressed by some of the current board members at the time they were chartered. Most of the school administrators, as well as the teachers union, were against the establishment of any new charter schools in the district.

Having just taken the position of superintendent three months earlier, and having come from one of the ten states that had not yet established charter schools, Brandon felt that he had a great deal to learn about this form of school choice. While working as an administrator in his former district, he had been an adjunct professor in a neighboring college. Teaching a course titled "Foundations of Education," he had used a textbook, *Teachers, Schools, and Society* by Sadker, Sadker, and Zittleman (2007). He knew that the new edition of the book contained background information on charter schools.

Turning to the book, Brandon learned that the charter school movement had begun in 1991 in Minnesota and that currently forty states along with the District of Columbia and Puerto Rico had established more than 3,500 schools that enrolled more than a million students. From the book he copied down his own notes concerning the characteristics that were common among charter schools. They included the following:

- Allow for the creation of a new or the conversion of an existing public school
- Prohibit admission tests
- Are nonsectarian
- Require a demonstrable improvement in performance
- Can be closed if they do not meet expectations
- Receive funding based on the number of students enrolled[1]

As he thought about charter schools in his district, he was aware that one of the chief arguments for charter schools was not a factor. Because the racial breakdown in the city was such that the student body was overwhelmingly made up of minority children, the hope that integration would occur proved to be a false hope. He was not sure about the other aspiration of improving student learning by reducing local and state regulations. In considering the testing data available, the success rate of charter schools was mixed. The Sadker and colleagues book also had concluded that the hoped-for innovation in these schools "is not happening." In fact, this source reported that "most charters . . . are mirroring the most traditional educational practices available."[2]

Critics also argue that charter schools tend to be spending more on administrative costs than regular public schools. On the other hand, the same textbook pointed out that "in other instances, charters were performing far better than other public schools, fueling a movement that has seen amazing growth."[3] While considering these conflicting statements, Brandon's thoughts returned to the strong opposition being expressed by the teachers' union. Jim Lazzeri, the president of the Riverdale Teacher Association would undoubtedly speak at the board meeting to oppose the resolution put forward by Jessica. He would probably quote a study on charter schools prepared by the national teachers union. Faculty members as well the board would be very interested in the superintendent's position on the resolution. There was another person who would notice his stand on the issue.

The previous week, Brandon had made his first trip to the state capital and had met with the newly elected governor and some of the leaders of the state legislature. He had learned that there were enough votes, at least in the upper house of the legislature, to raise the cap on the number of charter schools in the state. There certainly was no question that the governor supported the measure and would welcome the endorsement of the superintendent and the Board of Education of one of the largest districts in the state. On the other hand, to support the proposed resolution at the board meeting would undoubtedly disappoint the administrators and the faculty in his own district.

Other than Jessica, Brandon was not sure how the rest of the board members would vote on the resolution. Most of the board members had probably followed the progress of the current three charter schools in the city. Two of the three schools appeared to be doing quite well. The one that was faltering had experienced numerous problems. This school was operated by a for-profit company that was considering closing its doors even prior to the mandated five-year evaluation of the school.

In his reading, Brandon had learned that at least ten percent of the charter schools were being run by what were known as educational management organizations (EMOs). These companies saw charter schools as a way to gain public assistance for their schools. The entry of these corporations into the public school arena was a trend that made Brandon and many other public school educators very uneasy. This was especially true because of the wide-spread media coverage given to the Edison Project, which is the best known of the private companies engaged in public education. With approximately one hundred public schools located throughout the nation, the Edison Project has had a very uneven history.

In researching charter schools, Brandon learned that a study by Columbia University found that in many of these schools there was, "high teacher morale, enthusiasm for the curriculum, and satisfied parents."[4] At the same time, the study noted that, "some Edison employees reported that the company was hiding its problems from the public and that the needs of special education students, among others, were not being met." Other studies conducted by the American Federation of Teachers, National Education Association, and RAND Corporation found that Edison students were, "doing no better than regular public school students and sometimes worse."[5]

Brandon could not help but think that dealing with corporate executives of EMOs could be at least as difficult as his meetings with the state representatives of the teachers union. In any case, he had to prepare himself to speak at the meeting. It was likely that there would be a larger crowd than usual as Jim was bound to bring along a group of teachers. There was also a rumor circulating that Jessica had mobilized charter school parents to support her resolution. Of course there would be the usual reporters who would quote him in their accounts of the meeting. As a new superintendent, this would be his first test in dealing with a controversial agenda item.

## DISCUSSION QUESTIONS

1. What are your feelings about the following possible choice options?
   a. Open enrollment (a practice of allowing students to attend any public school within the district rather than their neighborhood school)
   b. Magnet schools (a public school which must follow all state and local regulations but has a specific academic focus)
   c. Charter schools
   d. A voucher system (government gives parents a voucher for a specific sum of money to allow their child to attend a public or private school in the school district)
2. What is your opinion of the current trend of granting charters to private companies to establish public schools?

3. If you were the superintendent of the Riverdale School District, what position would you take on the resolution to support the doubling of the number of charter schools in your state?

## NOTES

1. Sadker, Myra Pollack, David Miller Sadker, and Karen R. Zittleman, *Teachers, Schools, and Society* (Boston: McGraw-Hill, 2007), 145.
2. Sadker, Sadker, and Zittleman, *Teachers, Schools, and Society*, 147.
3. Sadker, Sadker, and Zittleman, *Teachers, Schools, and Society*, 147.
4. Sadker, Sadker, and Zittleman, *Teachers, Schools, and Society*, 149–150.
5. Sadker, Sadker, and Zittleman, *Teachers, Schools, and Society*, 150.

## ADDITIONAL RESOURCES

Carnoy, Mark, Rebecca Jacobsen, Lawrence Mishel, and Richard Rothstein. 2005. *The Charter School Dust-up: Examining the Evidence on Enrollment and Achievement.* Washington, DC: Economic Policy Institute; New York: Teachers College Press.

Dee, Thomas S., and Helen Fu. 2004. "Do Charter Schools Skim Students or Drain Resources?" *Economics of Education Review* 23: 259–271.

Kayes, Myron S., and Robert Maranto, eds. 2006. *A Guide to Charter Schools: Research and Practical Advice for Educators.* Lanham, MD: Rowman & Littlefield Education.

Kennedy, Mike. (2002). "Charter Schools: Treat or Boon to Public Schools." *American School & University* 75(4): 18–26.

National Alliance for Public Charter Schools. 2006. *Why Charter Schools?* April 9, 2007. http://www.publiccharters.org/section/introduction/.

Robelen, E. W. 2006. "Charters Harder to Get than Before, Suggests Survey of Authorizers." *Education Week* 25(36):14.

# Bullying, Is It Really
# That Big of a Problem?

*enforcing discipline*

**In recent years, the problem of bullying in schools has been given signifi-
cant attention. As a result, school districts and individual schools have actively sought to find effective ways to deal with the issue. In-service educational opportunities have been offered to increase the awareness of teachers
and administrators concerning the problem. At the same time, numerous
books and articles have appeared addressing the causes and effects of bullying. This case study deals with a principal who is considering doing something about bullying in his school.**

The parent who had visited him that morning had said that, "your head is in
the sand." He had claimed that there was significant bullying occurring at
every grade level in the Francis Parker Elementary School and that both the
principal and the faculty were "oblivious." As the principal of the school, Dr.
Gerald Kwikoski attempted to defend himself by answering that he had never
ignored it when he had received a disciplinary referral for bullying. Mr. John
Johnson, the parent, had not challenged his answer but rather suggested that
the professional staff didn't know what was going on in their school, or if they
did, many of them were ignoring it.

What troubled this parent was that his ten-year-old son, John Jr., had for the
past three weeks been the victim of verbal and even physical abuse by two
other boys in his class. John Jr. was small for his age and the two bigger boys
regularly called him, "the little squirt." The incident that prompted his father
to visit the principal occurred when the boy's teacher was out of the classroom. While the room was unattended, the two boys pushed young John into
a classroom closet while the rest of the students watched. They stood against
the door so that he was trapped in the closet. As the teacher was reentering

the room, they let him out, and the teacher merely asked John what he was doing in the closet.

John Sr. called the teacher and told him about the incident, explaining that this sort of thing had been going on for several weeks. The teacher assured him that he would watch the boys closely. After another episode occurred in the cafeteria, the boy's father decided to go directly to the principal. During their discussion, he had told Gerald that if things didn't change, he would be at the next school board meeting.

As a veteran principal, Gerald had been shaken by his meeting with John Sr. He knew that there had always been bullying in schools, but he had never seen it as a major problem in his school. He tried to think about how many incidents he had dealt with during his seventeen years as a school administrator. It seemed to him that there might have been as many as fifteen or twenty incidents each year. Most of them he thought he had handled quite well. On the other hand, he had heard that some of the local schools had seen bullying as an important enough issue to establish special programs to combat it.

He decided to go online to find out what he could learn. The first thing that amazed him was the unbelievable number of articles and books dealing with the problem. It was hard for him to know where to start. Because of the amount of material available, Gerald decided to randomly print out those articles that might be the most helpful. During the ensuing two hours he read a dozen different sources and was beginning to seriously question whether he had indeed been "oblivious."

Some statistics from an article published by the National Association of Secondary Principals had alarmed him. He had even taken notes on a section in an article titled, "Bullying: Facts for Schools and Parents."

- Bullying is the most common form of violence in our society; between 15 percent and 30 percent of students are bullies or victims.
- A recent report from the American Medical Association on a study of more than15,000 students in grades six through ten estimates that approximately 3.7 million youths engage in, and more than 3.2 million are victims of, moderate or serious bullying each year.
- Between 1994 and 1999, there were 253 violent deaths in school, 51 casualties were the result of multiple death events. Bullying is often a factor in school-related deaths.
- Membership in either bully or victim groups is associated with school dropout, poor psychosocial adjustment, criminal activity, and other negative long-term consequences.

- Direct, physical bullying increases in elementary school, peaks in middle school, and declines in high school. Verbal abuse, on the other hand, remains constant. The U.S. Department of Justice reports that younger students are more likely to be bullied than older students.
- More than two-thirds of students believe that schools respond poorly to bullying, with a high percentage of students believing that adult help is infrequent and ineffective.
- Twenty-five percent of teachers see nothing wrong with bullying or putdowns and consequently intervene in only 4 percent of bullying incidents.[1]

The last two bullets in his notes stuck with him. He did some quick math involving the fact that it was claimed that teachers only intervene in 4 percent of the bullying incidents. Of these interventions, he suspected that many of them may not have been reported to his office. If these numbers were true, it meant that there were literally hundreds of bullying situations in his school and that the vast majority of them were not being dealt with by the adults in the building.

Another article that caught his attention included a list of reasons why children became bullies. He had made some notes as well from this article.

- Frustration—a child is impaired in some way and is frustrated and resentful because the source of their difficulty has not been identified—problems can include deafness, dyslexia, autism, allergy, being left-handed, undiagnosed posttraumatic stress disorder, or some unidentified learning difficulty. Nevertheless, the child is expected to perform at the level required by the school, and no attempt is made to identify the source of the frustration.
- The child is being bullied, the responsible adults have repeatedly failed in their duty of care, so the child slowly and reluctantly starts to exhibit aggressive behaviors because that's the only way to survive in this bullying-entrenched climate.
- Poor or no role model— the child has no role model at home, or a poor role model for one or both parents and has never had the opportunity to learn behavior skills.
- Abuse at home—the child is being abused and is expressing their anger through bullying.
- Neglect at home—similar to abuse as the child's emotional and behavioral development is being retarded.
- Undue influence—the child has fallen in with the wrong crowd.
- Conduct disorder—the child has a conduct disorder, the precursor to antisocial, psychopathic, or other personality disorder.[2]

The third set of notes he had copied came from the first article published by the National Association of Secondary Principals, and it dealt with what schools can do about bullying.

- Early intervention. Researchers advocate intervening in elementary or middle school, or as early as preschool. Group and building-wide social skills training is highly recommended, as well as counseling and systematic aggression interventions for students exhibiting bullying and victim behaviors. School psychologists and other mental health personnel are particularly well equipped to provide such training as well as assistance in selecting and evaluating prevention programs.
- Parent training. Parents must learn to reinforce their children's positive behavior patterns and model appropriate interpersonal interactions. School psychologists, social workers, and counselors can help parents support children who tend to become victims as well as recognize bullying behaviors that require intervention.
- Teacher training. Training can help teachers identify and respond to potentially damaging victimization as well as to implement positive feedback and modeling to address appropriate social interactions. Support services personnel working with administrators can help design effective teacher training modules.
- Attitude change. Researchers maintain that society must cease defending bullying behavior as part of growing up or with the attitude of "kids will be kids." Bullying can be stopped! School personnel should never ignore bullying behaviors.
- Positive school environment. Schools with easily understood rules of conduct, smaller class sizes, and fair discipline practices report less violence. A positive school climate will reduce bullying and victimization.[3]

Obviously there were some options that he could consider for his school. He went on to read about several specific programs that had seemingly reduced bullying. Several weeks ago he had read an example of a school in his area that claimed success with their own unique approach to the problem in the local newspaper. It appeared from everything that he was reading that involving students needed to be an important part of any approach.

Gerald thought that perhaps the way to begin was to share at least some of what he had learned with the teachers in the school. He also wanted somehow to get an idea of what they felt about the extent of the problem in their building. Although he intended to follow through by talking with the teachers, he couldn't help but wonder how much the teachers really knew about the problem in their school. Maybe a better source of information would be his students.

It also occurred to him that some parents such as John Sr. could contribute to the search for a way to approach the issue. In the meantime, he had almost forgotten that his first priority had to be dealing with the boys who were picking on John Jr. After that he decided that he should come up with a plan of action.

## DISCUSSION QUESTIONS

1. Do you think that bullying is a bigger problem today than it has been in the past? Why? Why not?
2. Do you feel that it is true that the vast majority of incidents involving bullying go unreported or are ignored?
3. How should Gerald proceed in dealing with the problem in his school?

## NOTES

1. Andrea Cohn and Andrea Canter, "Bullying: Facts for Schools and Parents," *NASP Center*, http://www.nasponline.org/resources/factsheets/bullying_fs.aspx.

2. "Bullying in Schools," *School Bullying OnLine*, http://www.bullyonline.org/schoolbully/school.htm.

3. Cohn and Canter, "Bullying: Facts for Schools and Parents," 3.

## ADDITIONAL RESOURCES

Beaudoin, M.-N., and Maureen Taylor. 2004. *Breaking the Culture of Bullying and Disrespect, Grades K–8: Best Practices and Successful strategies.* Thousand Oaks, CA: Sage.

Fitzpatrick, K. M., Dulin, A. J., and Piki, B. F. 2007. "Not Just Pushing and Shoving: School Bullying among African American Adolescents." *Journal of School Health* 77: 16–22.

Geffner, R., Loring, M. T., and Young, C. 2001. *Bullying Behavior: Current Issues, Research and Interventions.* New York: Haworth Maltreatment & Trauma Press.

Gill, P. E., and Stenlund, M. A. 2005. "Dealing with a Schoolyard Bully: A Case Study." *Journal of School Violence* 4(4): 47–62.

Graham, S., Bellmore, A. D., and Mize, J. 2006. "Peer Victimization, Aggression, and Their Co-occurrence in Middle School: Pathways to Adjustment Problems." *Journal of Abnormal Child Psychology* 34: 349–364.

# Case Study 10

# Should We Let Them Print What They Want?

## *freedom of speech*

Freedom of speech and press is an essential ideal in our democratic system. Legislators and judges are entrusted with making decisions that define and, if necessary, restrict these rights. Media sources in our country have considerable latitude to criticize public officials and government policies. Historically, these freedoms have been limited for school newspapers, and recently there have been questions raised about the content of student Internet sites. Until 1988, courts had

> "made it clear that student literature enjoyed constitutional protection, and could only be regulated if it posed a substantial threat of school disruption, if it was libelous, or if it was judged vulgar, or obscene *after publication*. However, school officials could use 'prior censorship' and require students to submit literature before publication if such controls were necessary to maintain order in the school."[1]

In the Supreme Court case *Hazelwood School District v. Kuhlmeier* in 1988, the court, "gave public school officials considerable authority to censor school-sponsored student publications."[2] The decision stated that if the student newspaper was sponsored by the school as part of the curriculum, that school officials could exercise substantial control. Thus, if a journalism class was responsible for the student newspaper, it could definitely be regulated. It is less clear what rights administrators have in censoring school-sponsored publications that are not part of the curriculum. During the 1960s and 1970s, high schools also were forced to deal with a number of nonschool sponsored "underground" newspapers, which were often critical of school officials. Whether it be a regular school publication, one printed secretly, or student Web sites, administrators will undoubtedly be dealing with the issue of freedom of speech in the future.

Bob Lewis, one of the two assistant principals at Crossroads Senior High School had been upset earlier that day when he visited his boss, Principal Jason Kenyon. When he came in the office he was holding the first issue of the *Warrior*, which was the official student newspaper. He had taken forty-five minutes that morning to let off steam about a number of the statements in the paper. Perhaps most offensive was the phrase included in an editorial that referred to the "frequent inconsistent discipline policies of our assistant principals." For Bob, this was an unfair comment that implied that the administrators were making arbitrary decisions or possibly even playing favorites. No specific incidents were mentioned, only the general charge that the administrators were inconsistent in enforcing school rules.

There were several other sections of the publication that also were objectionable to Bob. There was a reference to Mildred Wittmeyer, an American history teacher, who it was suggested was a good teacher because she had lived through most of the history. Jason commented that Mildred would probably laugh at the statement and would not be all that upset because it said that she was a good teacher, even if she was considered ancient. Another teacher was criticized for her miniskirts, which were in style in the 1960s when the teacher "was in her prime." It went on to say that the skirts "didn't do much for her in the 21st century."

The female teachers were not the only ones criticized for their apparel. A male science teacher who always wore jeans and a flannel shirt to school was said to resemble a farmhand "milking cows in the barn." The varsity coach was judged to dress just fine, but his coaching strategy in the previous week's game was, "questionable." Secretly, Jason, who had been at the game, agreed with the student sportswriter. As he considered all of these entries into the school paper, he decided to look at his old school law book to determine what his legal rights were in regard to censoring school publications. What he saw is that materials that might be censored had to offer a substantial threat of school disruption or that materials had to be "vulgar," "obscene," or "libelous."

He was not sure that these descriptions fit any of the questionable passages. On the other hand, he suspected that some of his faculty and fellow administrators might well be upset by the paper. Knowing the students involved, especially the editors, he suspected that if he did nothing, future issues of the *Warrior* might be even more controversial. There was another complication that might surface. Hannah Bright, one of the co-editors, was the daughter of the publisher of the only daily newspaper in the city. Jason could not help but think that he might have an interest in how school officials reacted to his daughter's newspaper.

Although he was not as upset as his assistant principal, Jason agreed that they should talk to the faculty adviser about the paper. Anjali Hess was a twenty-three-year-old English teacher who was in her first year as the paper's faculty adviser. There had been little choice in appointing an adviser as Anjali was the only interested candidate for the position. Her background in the field was limited, although she did take one course in journalism and worked for a year on her college newspaper. Her predecessor was Mabel Larsen, who kept a tight rein on the students and had herself carefully edited every word that was printed in the newspaper.

After first period, they called Anjali down to discuss the newspaper. During that conversation, she was quite defensive about what the students had written. She informed Jason and Bob that she had cut a great deal out of the first drafts of their articles. She defended her students as good writers, some of whom had a "wicked sense of humor." When she cut out part of their drafts, the students had argued with her and one had even said that "she was not an adviser, she was a censor." Knowing about Mabel's reputation, Anjali asked her current staff members if any of them had worked with the previous adviser, and they all admitted they were new to the *Warrior* staff.

Because she expected that she might be called into the office about some of what was written in the issue, Anjali brought in an article from the *Seattle Times* about a law that was currently being debated in Congress. The article told of legislation that had been introduced by Rep. Dave Upthegrove (D–IA) "that would allow advisers to review student publication but strip them of any authority to control what is printed. Instead, students would be in charge of writing, editing, and publishing—and would be liable for any fallout."[3] The article pointed out that "laws in Arkansas, California, Colorado, Iowa, Kansas, Massachusetts, and Pennsylvania give students rights and responsibilities similar to those proposed by Upthegrove's bill."[4]

The congressman who proposed the law argued that it would, "generate an appreciation for constitutional rights and give young people a sense of civic responsibility."[5] Jason thanked Anjali for the article and suggested that there was likely to be some "fallout" from this issue and that she needed to be careful not to let students say things that might be hurtful in future issues. He ended the interview by saying that they would talk more about the newspaper before the next issue was published.

The discussion had not pacified the assistant principal who continued to scan the newspaper. Before he left Jason's office, Bob again exploded when he came upon a reference to the cheerleaders as the "rah-rah girls." This too did not seem like a major concern to Jason, yet he expected that there would be those who would question this and other statements in the paper. Already he had one administrator upset, and he would not be surprised if that afternoon he would be paid a visit by the basketball coach and maybe even the cheerleaders.

As he considered a course of action, one possibility that came to mind was just to ride out any furor over the newspaper and hope that the next issue was not so controversial. He could come down harder on the adviser but he knew she was a principled young woman who might resign from the extracurricular assignment rather than be considered a censor by the students. Another alternative would be to try to reason with the students. Such a tactic might be interpreted by them as intimidation. If they did, he might well hear from at least one powerful community member. The only thing that he was certain of was that he had to come up with some course of action before the next issue of the *Warrior* was published.

## DISCUSSION QUESTIONS

1. Should school administrators have the right to personally censor all school publications and Web sites established by school organizations?
2. Did you find the quotations from the student newspaper objectionable?
3. What should Jason do about his school's student newspaper?

## NOTES

1. Forrest W. Parkay and Beverly Hardcastle Stanford, *Becoming a Teacher* (Needham Heights: Pearson Education Company, 2001), 223.
2. Parkay and Stanford, *Becoming a Teacher*, 223.
3. Elliot Wilson, "Bill Would Free Student Press," *Seattle Times*, 21 January 2007, http://seattletimes.nwsource.com/html/education/2003534198_studentpress21m0.html.
4. Wilson, "Bill Would Free Student Press."
5. Wilson, "Bill Would Free Student Press."

## ADDITIONAL RESOURCES

Allen, Dan. 2005. "Fighting for Our Stories." *Advocate* 942: 26.
Dowling-Sendor, Benjamin 2003. "Stop the Presses?" *American School Board Journal* 190(10): 44–46.
Goodman, Mark. 2001. "Freedom of the Press Stops at the Schoolhouse Gate." *Nieman Reports* 55(1): 47–49.
Kopenhaver, Lillian L., and J. William Click. 2001. "High School Newspapers Still Censored Thirty Years after Tinker." *Journalism and Mass Communication Quarterly* 78: 321–339.
Selingo, Jeffrey. 2001, June 7. "Student Writers Try to Duck the Censors by Going Online." *New York Times*, G6.

# Training Rules

## *discipline policies*

Requiring student athletes to follow certain rules is not a new idea. Sometimes training rules are established by individual coaches, but more frequently, they are developed for all of the participants in a school's interscholastic sports program. Although the rules and penalties differ from school to school, all of them have in common the fact that they are difficult to enforce. Because the prohibited behaviors most often take place somewhere other than in the school building, these violations frequently go undetected or unreported. Along with prohibitions on the use of alcohol and cigarettes, more recently some schools have introduced mandatory drug testing for participants in their sports programs. Whatever the forbidden behavior, other students in the school are not subject to the same rules. For some, this double standard is unfair.

It had been a party for seniors only, and it had taken place after dark in a wooded area about a mile from the high school. From the accounts received by the school administration, there had been as many as forty students and at least four cases of beer. Anonymous sources had given Assistant Principal Larry Winckle many of the names of the students who were present. For the past three days, Larry had played detective and felt that he had definitively identified twenty-four names of senior class members who had participated in the party.

In talking with these students, some admitted they were there but denied they were drinking; others would not even confess to attending the party. By Wednesday, Larry lacked solid evidence that anyone had taken a drink at the party, despite the empty beer bottles that were found at the site. Among those students on his list were four varsity boys basketball players, three members of the girls basketball team, and two cheerleaders. Along with the athletes, it appeared that the student council president and the editor of the yearbook were also in attendance.

Word of the party had already spread to many parents as well as other community members. Because almost a week had gone by without any official action, there were rumors about a "cover-up." Larry's wife had heard it said at a local store that the school administration was afraid to punish the kids involved because they came from "influential" families. It was true that at least one board member's son had admitted being at the event but had claimed that he had not been drinking. Other community members were suggesting that the school officials were protecting their athletes because both the boys and girls varsity teams were in contention for league championships.

Neither theory was true, as both Larry and his boss Principal Carol Buckley wanted to enforce the school policy. The training rules for athletes stated that team members would not drink alcoholic beverages or smoke cigarettes during any season in which they were participating on a school team. The training rules also covered the cheerleading squad.

On Thursday morning, when she entered the office fifteen minutes before school started Carol was surprised to find nine students in her waiting room. They asked to talk with her, and she invited them into the office conference room. After everyone was seated, she asked Larry to join them. The first student to speak was the captain of the boys basketball team, Sam Wright. Sam ranked third academically in the senior class and had already been accepted at West Point.

Speaking for the group, he said that they had come that morning to tell the truth. Although several of them had drunk less than a full bottle of beer, the students present wished to confess that they had broken the training rules. In the case of one female basketball player, all of them had agreed that she had taken only one swallow of beer at the party. The administrators were also surprised when Sam also gave them a list of twenty-seven additional seniors who were at the party. He was quick to add that he could not say for certain that all of them had been drinking, but they certainly were all present. Accepting the list, Carol had asked the students whether Student Council President Jamie Lonergan or the Yearbook Editor Jeanne Carson had been drinking. After what seemed like a very long silence, he said in a soft voice, "yes, they were." Thanking the students for telling the truth, Carol wrote them passes for their first period classes.

Sitting back in his chair, Larry said to his boss, "We have problems." He took out of his jacket pocket the small student handbook and turned to the athletic training policy, which had been adopted by the school board several years earlier as a result of a similar drinking party. The policy required that all interscholastic athletes sign a pledge that they would not consume alcoholic beverages or smoke cigarettes while participating on a school team. Not only had the students signed the pledge, but the policy also required a parent signature. To determine whether they had a record of signed statements from all of the students, the principal called Sue Nelson, the school's athletic director, and asked him to bring the signed pledges to the office.

As soon as he arrived with the folder, a quick review of the forms made it clear that all of the confessing students and their parents had signed the forms. Sue read to them the section on the form that outlined the consequences for any violation of the policy. For the first offense, a student athlete was to be suspended from the team for two weeks. For both basketball teams that meant that the students involved would miss the next four games. These were games that would determine whether both of the squads would win their league championships. All but one of the students involved were in the starting lineup for their teams. If all of the guilty members of the boys varsity squad were suspended, the team would be down to only six players. This would be a major problem if several team members fouled out of a game. Larry, who frequently attended games, assured Carol that there were several junior varsity members who could join the varsity for the next four games.

The two administrators decided to take the rest of the morning to summon every student on the list given to them by the athletes. When these students were confronted with the fact that there had been eyewitness accounts of them drinking at the party, most, but not all, admitted that they were guilty. Those confessing included the student council president and the yearbook editor, who broke into tears as she explained how much stress she had been under in trying to meet the deadlines placed on the staff by the company that was publishing the yearbook. Sobbing, she had said because of this crisis, "we might not have a yearbook this year." After finding her tissue box for her, Carol had sent her back to class.

Before the two administrators could even talk about what to do next, the school's administrative assistant stuck her head in the door and told them that Ken Cummings, father of a senior on the girls basketball team, was on the phone and was rather vehement about talking with the principal. . . . They both knew Ken and were aware that he was a very opinionated fellow who had a temper. He had earlier in the year complained that the team's coach was ignorant of the fundamentals of basketball. Ken proceeded to criticize a number of the decisions made by the coach during the season. A careful scrutiny of his concerns made clear to the administrators that most of his complaints revolved around the fact that his daughter was not being properly used by the coach as she was too often on the bench.

Neither Carol nor Larry could guess why he was upset today, but they both suspected that his daughter, Sylvia, had already called her dad at home after her visit to the office with the other students. After a quick exchange of greetings, it was clear to Carol that Ken had heard about the confessions of the athletes. He angrily expressed his opinion that the whole policy was a "crock" and that a couple of swigs of beer taken by some eighteen-year-old kids should not result in throwing away league championships or permanently damaging the reputations of some "great kids."

He admitted that he had signed the "damn form" but he wanted "you guys to know that you better not just punish the athletes." He said that he had heard that the student council president was the one that brought the beer to the party. Carol did not stop Ken long enough to tell him that the training policy only covered athletes. Students participating in other extracurricular activities had not signed any forms, nor had their parents. After she ended the phone call, Carol knew that hearing about this double standard would only further infuriate the parent. It also would not alter Ken's opinion that all the students involved should be equally punished. It did not take much imagination to foresee his attendance at the next Board of Education meeting. He had taken his complaints to these meetings in the past.

In this case, Carol had some sympathy with Ken's views. She could recall that the training policy had been written to eliminate partying by the school's athletes. When the rules were brought up, no one had considered extending them to students participating in other school activities. If every extracurricular club member was held to the same rules, more than half of the students in the school would be included. As an administrator, she wondered if a policy that attempted to monitor the outside activities of close to a thousand students was even enforceable. On the other hand, in defense of the current policy, such training rules were used for college athletic programs as well as in high schools throughout the country. Her school was not the only institution with a double standard.

In thinking about the issue before her, Carol remembered a discussion at a recent county principals' meeting about the possibility of mandating drug testing for all high school athletes. This was a whole new area where charges of a double standard would undoubtedly emerge. Adoption of such a policy was not imminent in their county, but it might well be a possibility in the future. In any case, they needed to concentrate on their current dilemma.

As they considered their options, Larry suggested that it would be appropriate to at least inform the superintendent. He suggested that, "we don't want her to learn about this issue from an angry parent." Before she called her boss, Carol wanted to develop her own strategy. As the high school principal, she felt that this was primarily her problem.

# DISCUSSION QUESTIONS

1. Is it a good idea for high school athletic programs to develop training rules that attempt to stop student athletes from smoking or drinking alcoholic beverages? Why or why not?
2. Should such policies be extended to require athletes to undergo drug testing? Why or why not?
3. Should these policies be applied to participants in other extracurricular activities? Why or why not?
4. What should Carol and Larry do about the situation described in this case study?
   a. Should they suspend all of the athletes involved for the two weeks that is required by the policy? Why or why not?
   b. Should they punish any other students for participating in the party? Why or why not?
   c. What should they do about the students who did not confess their participation but were included on the list provided by the athletes?

# ADDITIONAL RESOURCES

Brendtro, Larry K., and Gordon A. Martin, Jr. 2006. "Respect Versus Surveillance: Drug Testing Our Students." *Reclaiming Children and Youth* 15(2): 75–81.

Dowling-Sendor, Benjamin 2002. "'Reasonable' Drug Testing." *American School Board Journal* 189(9): 76, 78, 80.

Finn, Kristin V., and H. Jeannette Willert. 2006. "Alcohol and Drugs in Schools: Teachers' Reactions to the Problem." *Phi Delta Kappan* 88(1): 37–40.

Gehring, John. 2005. "Parents Sue Ohio District over Beer Drinking on Trip." *Education Week* 23(34): 4.

Mawdsley, Ralph D., and Charles J. Russo. 2003. "The Supreme Court Upholds Drug Testing of Student Participants in Extracurricular Activities." *School Business Affairs* 69(2): 48–52.

# The Need for Parental Involvement

## *gaining parental support*

The homes that our school children come from each day are varied and in many ways different from the homes of children of previous generations. One need only to consider the following statistics to understand some of these changes.

- Only two-thirds of American children now live in two-parent homes. (Only 35 percent of black non-Hispanic children live in such homes.)
- The number of unmarried opposite or same-sex partners living together has more than doubled. Significant numbers of our children are coming from this type of home.
- In 1960, fewer than half of the married women with children between the ages of six and seventeen worked outside the home. Approximately 80 percent of these mothers work outside the home today. The change has been even greater for married women with children younger than age six. It has gone from one in five to three in five.
- The number of so called "latchkey" children has increased dramatically. On average these children are watching television 25 hours per week.
- Half of new marriages now end in divorce.
- One in five American children are living in poverty. (This includes 33 percent of black children and 29 percent of Hispanic children.)
- An estimated 1 million American children are homeless.
- One-third of American high school students drop out of school.
- Twenty percent of high school students and ten percent of middle school students admit to using "illicit drugs."
- During the past twenty-five years suicides of those between age fifteen and twenty-four have tripled. [1]

When one considers these statistics, the goal of increasing the level of cooperation between the school and a student's home life becomes even more crucial.

It had started with an article in the *Christian Science Monitor.* The headline, which read "Schools Strive for 'No Parent Left Behind,'" was the first thing that caught his attention. Stacy A. Teicher, the staff writer who wrote the story, began by referring to the provision of the No Child Left Behind legislation that allowed parents of students in schools that were "chronically failing academically" to seek tutoring for their children or to transfer them to other schools in the district. She went on to point out that this was not having a major impact in failing schools, as parents of only one percent of eligible students chose to transfer their children and only nineteen percent accepted the supplemental tutoring that was available in the 2003–2004 school year.[2]

After the reference to No Child Left Behind, the article focused on the need to make parents partners with the school in any efforts to help students raise their level of academic achievement. The author argued that family members should be "allies" in any school improvement plan. To illustrate her point, Teicher cited research studies that supported the idea that parental involvement could improve academic achievement.[3]

As he thought about it, Superintendent Bill Ennis knew that the article was probably correct in placing a high value on the need for schools to work with parents. His fifteen years experience as a teacher, building principal, and now a superintendent had taught him that if a teacher could get children reading at home with their parents and if the school offered encouragement and perhaps training, parents could help students with all of their homework. In considering the importance of the home environment, it occurred to him that with many Asian American students he had known, the parents' commitment to education was a chief factor in the success of these children. It seemed to follow that if other racial and ethnic groups adopted a similar attitude concerning the importance of academic improvement, then it would indeed make a difference.

As the new superintendent of the Henderson School District, he had been considering what he should present to the board as his educational goals for the coming year. One of these goals could be to create a more active relationship between the school and parents. Prior to making such a recommendation he needed to figure out what this would mean in his community. The district was geographically quite large but was rather lightly populated. At one time it was primarily made up of small farms. Following the construction of an exit off a major highway out of a nearby mid-sized city, community leaders expected that Henderson would become a new suburb. This growth had never occurred in the past, in part because many commuters did not want to pay for the gas that would be necessary for the thirty minute ride into the city.

Not only did the Henderson district not grow, it had begun to lose population. Many of the small farms ceased to exist, and most adults living in the district were either commuting to jobs in the suburbs or the city. Large numbers of these residents were working in blue collar occupations and in most families, both parents worked full-time jobs. The community was anything but prosperous.

When he and his wife had first visited Henderson for his interview with the Board of Education, they were both taken aback by the seemingly high level of poverty in the community. Especially obvious were the conditions of the businesses on Main Street. At least one-quarter of the commercial buildings seemed to be unoccupied. Unfortunately, less than twenty percent of the teachers and administrators chose to live in the district, and therefore their children were attending neighboring schools. Only one of the three principals had purchased a home in Henderson. As the new superintendent, Bill had been strongly encouraged to live in the community. After four months, he and his family were beginning to feel at home. The people had been very friendly and each day he was meeting new parents and community members. The last superintendent had chosen to live outside the community, and Bill felt many people were glad that he had decided to become one of their neighbors and to send his children to the Henderson schools.

After reading the article, Bill decided to look at some other sources dealing with parental involvement. He had been influenced in college when he read for an assignment what his professor had said was a crucial document in the educational reform movement that was continuing into the twenty-first century. The *Nation at Risk Report* had highlighted the role of parents by giving them specific instructions. Bill thought that these were important enough that he looked them up and made a copy. The recommendations were as follows:

- Parents "must possess a deep respect for intelligence, achievement and learning and skills needed to use them."
- Parents have the "right to demand the best from schools and colleges."
- Parents are a child's "first and most influential teacher," and they must be a "living example of what you expect your child to honor and emulate."
- Parents must nurture their "child's curiosity, creativity and confidence and be active participants in the work of schools."
- Parents themselves must be lifelong learners.
- Parents must model "intellectual and moral integrity coupled with hard work and commitment."[4]

He also copied another source that he had come across. It argued that the most accurate predictor of a student's achievement in school is not income or social status, but the extent to which a student's family is able to:

- create a home environment that encourages learning;
- express high (but not unrealistic) expectations for their children's achievement and future careers;
- become involved in their children's education at school and in the community.[5]

The same article outlined characteristics of families whose children were doing well in school. He had also thought these were worthy of copying.

- Establish a Daily Family Routine.

   Examples: Provide time and a quiet place to study; assign responsibility for household chores; be firm about times to get up and go to bed; have dinner together

- Monitor Out-of-School Activities

   Examples: Set limits on TV; check up on children when parents are not at home; arrange for after-school activities and supervised care

- Model the Value of Learning, Self-Discipline, and Hard Work

   Examples: Communicate through questioning and conversation; Demonstrate that achievement comes from working hard; use reference materials and the library

- Express High But Realistic Expectations for Achievement

   Examples: Set goals and standards that are appropriate for the children's age and maturity; recognize and encourage special talents; inform friends and family about successes

- Encourage Children's Development and Progress in School

   Examples: Maintain a warm and supportive home; show interest in children's progress at school; help with homework; discuss the value of a good education and possible career options; stay in touch with teachers and school staff

- Encourage Reading, Writing, and Discussion among Family Members

   Examples: Read, listen to children read, and talk about what is being read; discuss the day over dinner; tell stories and share problems; write letters, lists, and messages [6]

There was plenty of advice in the literature about what schools could do to encourage parents to become more engaged in their children's education. One set of instructions that caught his attention was included in a book written by

Laurence Steinberg. The author recommended that, in the United States, we need to:

- transform the national debate over the causes and cures of our achievement problem from one about reforming schools to one about changing students' and parents' attitudes and behaviors.
- make it clear in the minds of young people and parents that the primary activity of childhood and adolescence is schooling. If we want children and teenagers to value education and strive for achievement, adults must behave as if doing well in school—not just finishing school, but actually doing well in school—is more important than socializing, more important than organized sports, more important than working at after school jobs, and more important than any other activity in which young people are involved.
- have a serious and open discussion about the high rate of parental irresponsibility in this country and the toll it is taking on youngsters' lives. Parenting skills must be taught in well-designed programs that can be sponsored by schools.
- encourage schools to expand their efforts to actively draw parents into school programs. This will require restructuring and rescheduling school programs to meet the needs of working parents.[7]

Another source that impressed him was an article in a journal called *School Improvement Research*. This article included some ideas Bill thought might be helpful in his district. He would urge families to:

- work directly with children in the home by reading with them, "supporting work on homework assignments" and actually tutoring them using instructions and materials supplied by the teacher.
- support school activities by attending parent–teacher conferences, open houses, volunteering in the classroom and on field trips, and communicating directly with the teacher by phone or through notes.
- ensure that effective programs offering parental involvement have an orientation or training component.
- make certain that schools offer a wide range of opportunities for parental involvement because of the various schedules, interests, and abilities of parents.[8]

Although he was excited about the challenge of increasing parental involvement, he understood that it would not be easy. This was especially true because of the many children in the district who came from what might be considered "disadvantaged homes." These low-income parents faced a number of issues that might prevent their involvement with schools. Some of these factors were listed in another article that he had read.

- Lack of time or energy (due to long hours of heavy physical labor, for example)
- Embarrassment or shyness about one's own educational level or linguistic ability
- Lack of understanding or information about the structure of the school and accepted communication channels
- Perceived lack of welcome by teachers and administrators
- Teachers and administrators' assumptions of parents' disinterest or inability to help with children's schooling.[9]

Armed with the results of his research, Bill began to think about what he might recommend in the Henderson School District. Before formalizing the initiative, he would have to convince his fellow administrators as well as the faculty of the need for such an effort. Because most of them did not live in the district, at present there was only limited contact between parents and teachers. Each month, the local chapter of the Parent–Teacher Association might draw anywhere between twenty to fifty people depending on the program. Although Bill and his principals usually attended, no more than a handful of parents and teachers usually attended. The group had several fundraising activities every year, the proceeds of which were used for selected school programs.

There was also an open house in every school building each fall. The kindergarten open house always drew close to 100 percent of parents. After that, attendance gradually dwindled and by the time students reached the high school level, the open house was sparsely attended. Bill was aware that the elementary school also had parent conferences at the end of the first quarter. Attendance at these events was only fair because most of the timeslots for conferences were during the day, when parents were working. During the recent contract negotiations, the faculty union had agreed that the elementary teachers would be available for evening appointments for one night.

In addition, some of the elementary teachers attempted to have ongoing communication with the parents either with their own class newsletter, telephone calls, or sometimes e-mail. Beyond that, the only communication from the school came when a student was in trouble. Bill was not aware of administrators or teachers communicating positive accomplishments of any students. He remembered in his previous district a principal who made "happy calls." A teacher would give the principal the name of a student who was showing academic improvement or who had done an outstanding project. That evening the administrator would call the parent to commend the student. Both the parent and the student were usually delighted with the call, and it was also something that the principal enjoyed doing. Perhaps this was one idea he could pursue. If it were not the principal, the teachers might make their own "happy calls."

He realized that many of the teachers knew very little about the district in which they were working. Eighty percent of the faculty drove the half-mile from the exit on the freeway and seldom, if ever, traveled the back roads where the children lived. His own tours of the community had certainly helped him better understand the district. He had read about a school that, as part of the new teacher orientation, had given new faculty and staff members a two-hour school bus tour of the district. Perhaps he would try this idea out on the administrators and some faculty members.

Before talking to anyone else, Bill thought that he should better organize his thinking. As a new first-time superintendent, he had never launched a districtwide project. He was sure that he needed the support of the other administrators and the faculty and, at some point, the Board of Education would need to be included in the planning. There was also the issue of parents. Should he attempt to use the rather weak PTA, or should he look for another approach to reach the parents?

The more he thought about a process for introducing his initiative, the more complicated things seemed to become. On the other hand, he knew that this was an opportunity for leadership. It was the reason he had become a school administrator. The cause was one that he believed in and now all he had to do was to find a way to accomplish his objective.

## DISCUSSION QUESTIONS

1. List several ways that teachers and schools can communicate with parents and engage them in their children's education.
2. How can school districts better involve disadvantaged and minority parents who have not chosen to participate in the opportunities being offered by the district?
3. Outline a possible plan Bill could use to carry out his initiative of gaining additional parental engagement in their children's education.

## NOTES

1. Myra Pollack Sadker, David Miller Sadker, and Karen R. Zittleman, *Teachers, Schools, and Society* (Boston: McGraw-Hill, 2007), 191–200.

2. Stacy A. Teicher, "Schools Strive for 'No Parent Left Behind,'" *The Christian Science Monitor*, February 15, 2007, http://www.csmonitor.com/2007/0215/p13s02-legn.html.

3. Teicher, "Schools Strive for 'No Parent Left Behind.'"

4. U.S. Department of Education, National Commission on Excellence in Education, *A Nation at Risk: The Imperative for Educational Reform*, 1983, A Word to Parents and Students, 7.

5. San Diego County Office of Education, "Parent Involvement and Student Achievement," *Notes From Research*, http://www.sdcoe.net/lret2/family/pia.html.

6. San Diego County Office of Education, "Parent Involvement and Student Achievement," 3–6.

7. Laurence Steinberg, *Beyond the Classroom* (New York: Simon & Schuster, 1996), 188.

8. Kathleen Cotton and Karen Reed Wikelund, "Parent Involvement in Education," *School Improvement Research*, http://www.nwrel.org/scpd/sirs/3/cu6.html.

9. Cotton and Wikelund, "Parent Involvement in Education," 6.

## ADDITIONAL RESOURCES

Cooper, Carey E., and Robert Crosnoe. 2007. "The Engagement in Schooling of Economically Disadvantaged Parents and Children. *Youth & Society* 38: 372–391.

Drummond, Kathryn V., and Deborah Stipek. 2004. "Low-Income Parents' Beliefs about Their Role in Children's Academic Learning." *Elementary School Journal* 104:197–213.

Jeynes, William H. 2003. "A Meta-Analysis: The Effects of Parental Involvement on Minority Children's Academic Achievement." *Education and Urban Society* 35: 202–219.

"NCLB Rules for Parent Involvement." 2007. *Gifted Child Today* 30(1): 6.

Rogers, John. 2006. "Forces of Accountability? The Power of Poor Parents in NCLB." *Harvard Educational Review* 76: 611–641.

Souto-Manning, M., and Swick, K. J. (2006). Teachers' beliefs about parent and family involvement: Rethinking our family involvement paradigm. *Early Childhood Education Journal*, 34, 187–193.

# Do We Really Have a Free Public Education?

## *fundraising*

**Since the emergence of the so-called common school in the mid-nineteenth century, we, in the United States, have prided ourselves in the fact that every child is able to attend a free public school in his or her community. Beginning with the leadership of Horace Mann in Massachusetts, every state developed free elementary schools. As the nineteenth century ended, private secondary schools were converted into public high schools, thus completing the process of establishing a total public education system. These free public schools became an American institution that brought together students from every economic class, ethnic group, and race. Perhaps the most important characteristic of our education system was that it was publicly supported and even the poorest children could attend without cost to their family. With the limited school budgets and numerous extracurricular activities of today, however, parents frequently find that there now are mandatory and voluntary expenses related to their children's education.**

It was ironic that the issue emerged during a discussion at a fundraising dinner held at the Lutheran church. The church's youth group was raising money for a mission's trip to New Orleans to help with the ongoing cleanup activity. James Thompson, as superintendent of schools of the Pine Hills Central School, often was approached to attend such affairs. As a middle-class suburban community with many churches and civic groups, it was not unusual that he and his wife would attend such charity events quite frequently. In reality, they rather enjoyed the occasions, especially the dinners, where the food was usually of excellent quality.

It was also common for him to be part of conversations concerning the school district. Some people welcomed the opportunity to share their thoughts about the schools directly with the superintendent. Although at times this was a mixed blessing, James generally appreciated the opportunity to know what people were thinking. Administrators who live outside their school districts often miss this kind of "grassroots" input.

Last evening at the dinner, he heard about an issue that he had not thought about for some time. He and his wife sat at a table with four other couples, all of whom were parents of children attending schools in the district. After going through the serving line, everyone at the table was beginning to enjoy their dinner when a father asked if any of them were going to attend a spaghetti dinner next week. James had already purchased tickets as it was a fundraiser to help the high school band earn enough money to march in the Cotton Bowl parade. As a member of the Band Booster Club, the father who had raised the issue took the opportunity to sell tickets to the other parents sitting at the table.

Another parent at the table then mentioned the fundraising drive that was under way to help finance a trip by the baseball team to Florida during the spring break. The trip would offer the team an opportunity to play against some southern high schools long before they were able to begin practice on their home field in Massachusetts. A mother who had a son on the team was taking orders for large bags of popcorn and kettle corn. While doing so, she announced to the table that this fundraiser was very popular, and people really enjoyed the popcorn. She proudly shared with the others that the team had already raised over two thousand dollars on the sale. Although she wasn't aware of the profit margin, she was glad that any profits would help reduce the cost of the trip for the team members.

The same parent also brought up the middle school student council's project to raise money to buy toys and books for the local children's hospital. Everyone at the table agreed that such service projects provided a great experience for kids. A parent who had been very quiet thus far during the discussion observed that being a parent these days was an "expensive proposition." His wife joined the conversation by suggesting that it wasn't just the older kids who cost money. She went on to share the fact that her two elementary school children were each given a list of recommended school supplies during the first week of classes. Even shopping at a local discount store, it had cost her over a hundred dollars to buy those items recommended for the children. James became a bit uncomfortable when the lady went on to say, "and I thought our children were supposed to be receiving a free public education."

The concerns kept coming when the two couples with students in the senior class began to compare notes. They talked about the cost of fees required with each college application. One parent talked about the four trips the family had already taken to visit colleges to which their son had applied. Three of the trips required the family to pay for motel rooms as well as two days of meals. Another parent mentioned the tuition they were paying for their daughter to take an SAT preparation course at the local community college.

The mother of one of the seniors reported that her son was working fifteen hours a week to earn money to help pay for some of the expenses but most of his money was going to keeping his car on the road. The parents agreed that a high school student having a car was a mixed blessing, but conceded that the part-time job that the car made possible was probably a valuable learning experience.

The discussion really heated up when the group turned to the topic of the senior prom. The mother of a senior girl who had graduated the previous year mentioned the cost of the prom dress, accessories, and the trip to the beauty parlor to get her hair and nails done. There was also the boutonniere and at least an offer to help pay for the ticket and the limousine. A father who had had a son attend a recent prom was willing to bet that his boy spent more money than his date.

At that point the parents began to reminisce about their own senior proms. One of them recalled that his parents had driven him and his date to the dance. None of them could remember any food connected with the dance and certainly not a dinner. All but one of the adults at the table had attended proms that were held in the school gym rather than at a fancy hotel. There seemed to be agreement at the table that the "prom thing" had gotten out of hand.

By the time they had eaten their desserts, James had heard enough. It was clear to him that his school district was engaged in a large number of programs and events that were costing parents money. Probably the people at this dinner table could afford these extra expenses, but he knew that there were significant numbers of parents in the district who might be having trouble making ends meet.

Riding home after the dinner, James and his wife, Molly, reflected on what, if anything, the school district could do about the extra expenses that might well be burdening some of the parents in the community. It occurred to him that he should consider a way to somehow control the number of fundraisers that school organizations could carry on each year. At least they could try to develop a schedule so that the community was not bombarded with so many of these projects at one time. He didn't know who in the district could be assigned to try to schedule and perhaps limit fundraisers.

One way to do it was to force groups to gain the permission of the Board of Education but the agendas for these meetings were already overcrowded. Board members might also see this as an administrative function. With so many projects going on in the seven schools that made up the district, it would be a job for any one of his staff to try to monitor them.

Along with the events and fundraising drives, there was also the issue of school supplies. He wondered if it was really realistic to require parents to purchase items such as student notebooks, compasses, and rulers. It also occurred to him that the high school was requiring students to purchase graphing calculators that cost approximately eighty dollars. Some of the athletes' families were spending large amounts of money on athletic footwear. There also was a lab fee for art classes.

Of all of these issues it seemed that the cost of the proms was causing the most concern. He wondered how many students were forced to forego attendance because of the cost involved. He was sure that only about half the senior class was attending the dance. Maybe the senior class should be expected to raise more money to reduce the ticket cost. Such a requirement would probably just lead to more fundraisers. He knew that it was not appropriate to ask the taxpayers to help pay for the dance by putting an appropriation in the school budget. Although bringing the event back to the high school gym was a possibility, he could only guess at the reaction of the senior class if he were to suggest such a move. There were no easy answers to any of the issues, and the dinner conversation would continue to plague him.

## DISCUSSION QUESTIONS

1. Should school districts attempt to regulate fundraising projects initiated by school organizations? If so, how?
2. Should parents be expected to purchase school supplies? What items should parents of students be asked to purchase? What school supplies should be the responsibility of the school district?
3. Have prom expenses become excessive? What, if anything, can school districts do about these costs?
4. What, if anything, should James do in his district about the issues raised at the dinner table?

## ADDITIONAL REFERENCES

Foster, Kristin. 2000. "Bringing School Fundraising and Procurement to the Web." *Technology & Learning* 21(2): 36–37.

Greifner, Laura. 2006. "Indiana Court Strikes Down Mandatory Fees." *Education Week* 25(31): 5.

Holzberg, Carol. 2005. "A Web Tour: Grassroots Fundraisers, Deals, and Discounts." *Technology & Learning* 25(11): 68–70.

Statz, Bambi L. 2000. "Escalating Student Fees: Do They Treat Students and Tax-payers Equitably? *School Business Affairs* 66(8): 17–23.

Struck, Myron. (2001). "Easy Money? The Fuzzy Math of Online Fund-Raising." *American School Board Journal* 188(1): 24–26.

Wassmer, Robert W., and Ronald C. Fisher. 2002. "Interstate Variation in the Use of Fees to Fund K–12 Public Education. Economics of Education Review 21: 87–100.

# Gifted and Talented Education Program?

*funding gifted programs*

**As a nation, we spend huge amounts of money on the education of students with disabilities. Both the federal and state governments provide significant financial assistance to local school districts for these required programs. There is no such mandate or large aid programs for the education of gifted and talented students. If a school district wants to offer such programs, most often the money must come from the local taxpayers. When a district seeks to reduce its local tax burden, it is almost impossible to save money by cutting services for the students in special education programs, as they are tightly regulated by both the state and federal governments. The same is not true of gifted and talented programs operated by a local district. Such offerings are often vulnerable when budget cuts are necessary. This is the situation in the following case study.**

Superintendent John Phillips wished that his two elementary principals Sarah Martin and Ben Coughlin could agree on the value of the gifted and talented program in their schools. The fact was that these two administrators often disagreed with each other on many subjects. Although John had only worked with them for two years as the superintendent of the Midlakes Central School District, both Sarah and Ben had been principals of their respective schools for more than ten years. Both in their own way were effective as a building administrator, but they were still very different.

Sarah was a former sixth grade teacher in the district, who was known as a wonderful instructor. While in the classroom, she had maintained high academic expectations for her students and as a result, they had always done quite well on the year-end examinations. She also was known as a creative teacher who had been able to find exciting and unique ways to engage her students. Perhaps it was this interest in teaching methods that caused her to admire the work of Carol Porter. Carol was the instructor in Sarah's school who had developed, what was in her principal's mind, a model "pull-out" program for gifted and talented students in grades three through six. Twice a week for fifty minutes, children identified as gifted at their grade level would go to Carol's classroom for a lesson designed to enrich their curriculum. The activities ranged from unique science experiments to research assignments that required students to circulate questionnaires to their family as well as to other members of the community. For the students who were lucky enough to be chosen, most found their "pull-out" experience to be one of their favorite school activities.

Even though it seemed to be a program that was well received in the district, it presented some difficulties. At times, parents questioned the way students were selected to participate. It had taken a number of years, but the school now used a formula that considered IQ scores, student grades, and teacher recommendations. However, it seemed that no matter how the students were selected, there were always a few parents who questioned the process. There were also teachers who had commented that, by the fifth and sixth grade, those students who had been in the program since third grade had often formed a social clique as a result of the friendships that had developed. At least in one class, some of the other students called these kids "the brains." Each year there also had been a teacher or two who had complained that taking their "best and brightest" students out of social studies and science classes denied the teacher and the remaining students the intellectual stimulation that these children provided for the class.

Despite these criticisms, there was little question that Carol was a popular member of the faculty. For Sarah, Carol's program was one that she felt was essential, as she had long been committed to providing something special for those outstanding students who might otherwise become bored or disinterested in school. She saw these students as the future leaders, scientists, and scholars of the next generation. Many times in conversations, she had compared what was being spent on special education and remediation to the miniscule investment in gifted and talented students. It was not that she begrudged the special advantages given to children with disabilities, but she fervently believed that they needed to do more for their most able students.

Ben, on the other hand, had been a Title I remedial math instructor in the district a dozen years ago. When he was appointed principal at the William Seward Elementary School, the gifted and talented program in the school had only been in existence for two years. The teacher was Samantha Curtis, whom Ben had known as a faculty colleague in the school. Although they had been fellow teachers, they had not been close friends, and Samantha had privately voiced to several other faculty members her opinion that Ben "was not smart enough to be a principal." Ben heard about Samantha's comment from a friend, but he had tried very hard not to hold it against her.

There was no question that Samantha had developed what most of the faculty considered a solid pull-out program. In addition to her classroom duties, she was a past president of the local teachers' union and had remained the union representative in her building. Through the years, she had been in Ben's office acting as a spokesperson of the union, often as a representative when there was a personnel problem in the school. She had also been a spokesperson in several grievance hearings that involved the principal. In addition, Ben had dealt with her when she complained about several classroom teachers who were not cooperating fully in releasing their students for the pull-out program. All of these contacts had been conducted in a professional manner, but there still had not emerged anything like a true friendship. Although he probably would not even admit it to himself, Ben would not have been all that unhappy if Samantha ceased to be a faculty member in his building.

On several occasions during the past decade when the district was facing a budget crisis, some suggested that the program for gifted and talented children was an "unnecessary frill." During these discussions, Ben and other members of the administration had been supportive of the program and kept it in the budget. The last time this had occurred, the Board of Education chose instead to eliminate the high school orchestra along with the entire string program. The current suggestion about cutting the gifted and talented program had been made recently at a meeting of the board's budget committee. Prior to the meeting, the full board had made clear to the superintendent that there would be no additional faculty and staff in next year's budget, in large part because the district had been losing students the past three years.

The district was able to maintain the workforce despite the fact that there were ten percent less students. At the last budget committee session, two custodial positions and one job in the high school office were eliminated as the individuals in these roles were retiring. There had been additional suggestions of personnel cuts that might need to be made. It was now only ten days until the board would have to adopt a final budget for the coming year. At this stage of the preparation, there had been no decision that would lead to the reduction of the teaching staff.

Reducing class size had been a major goal in the district for the last five years. As a result of this initiative, it had developed a policy that mandated that classes in grades K through three should not exceed eighteen students. Beginning in the fourth grade, the Midlakes Central Schools had chosen to cap the enrollment at twenty-four. If those limits were to be maintained for the coming year, it would be impossible to eliminate any regular teaching positions. John knew that the previous superintendent had convinced the board that this class-size initiative would eventually lead to higher test scores. Unfortunately this had not yet occurred.

At the board meeting prior to the recent budget committee session, John reported on the most recent test scores. The scores on the examinations given in grades three through eight had declined in each of the past two years. When asked by a committee member what needed to be done to raise these scores at the elementary level, Ben answered that his school could use another remedial reading teacher to work with the failing students. The board member raising the question reminded the committee that the entire board had agreed that there would be no new faculty positions. At this point, another committee member commented that there must be something that they could cut.

This question led to a rehashing of the decision that had been made to end the string program. The board members had expected a great public outcry. Initially, there had been a number of unhappy parents, but the uproar had soon calmed down, and the community seemed to accept the decision. Another veteran member of the committee recalled an earlier decision to cut the driver education elective. This led the individual who had suggested making cuts to hire remedial reading teachers to ask, "how about that program that the union leader runs?" Ben said, "You mean Mrs. Curtis. She teaches our pull-out program for gifted children."

Following this suggestion, an extended discussion followed. Sarah Martin strongly defended the need for the gifted and talented offering. John also talked about the importance of providing special services for these children. During this discussion, Ben was quiet until he was asked directly for his opinion. His answer was that he didn't want to cut any faculty, but if forced to choose, the gifted and talented program would be high on his list. When asked if he really believed that a remedial reading teacher would make a difference, he assured the group that such a position would be extremely helpful in raising the reading scores of a number of the failing students.

The committee session ended with at least two of the board members seriously considering the option of hiring a remedial reading teacher for each elementary school with the understanding that the gifted program would be eliminated. These board members said that this idea should be taken to the full board for consideration at the next meeting. After the meeting, when just the administrators were left in the room, Sarah verbally attacked her fellow elementary principal for not defending the gifted program. When Ben tried to defend himself by saying he had not supported cutting the program, she went on to charge him with letting his personal dislike of Samantha get in the way of his responsibility to the students. With the level of tension rising in the room, John cut off the discussion and said that they would consider this issue at their administrative meeting on Friday.

After everyone left the district office, John sat at his desk thinking about the upcoming budget decision. He knew that his first challenge would be to get his administrative team to agree on a course of action. It was the practice in the district to have all four building principals present at board meetings. The last thing he wanted was public discord in his administrative team. It appeared now that any differences between them would have to be dealt with at the administrative meeting. It was possible that the middle school principal, high school principal, or the business manager would have some ideas about saving money. In the meantime, he needed to do something about the conflict between his two principals.

Even before that, it was important for him to clarify his own thoughts about cutting the gifted and talented program to provide remedial reading teachers. Like the principals, he was very sensitive to the need to raise test scores but he also knew that there might well be significant support among faculty and parents for the gifted and talented program. It occurred to him that the teachers' union could also be upset with such a decision. Yet he realized that the two teachers currently providing the program would not be eliminated as faculty members in the district. It would be two newly hired teachers who would lose their jobs given the fact that staff layoffs were always based on a teacher's seniority in a tenure area. After thinking about all of these issues, John decided to begin his preparation for the upcoming meetings by doing some reading about the education of gifted and talented students.

## DISCUSSION QUESTIONS

1. Do you feel that "pull-out" programs are a good way to serve gifted students at the elementary level? Why or why not?
2. Do you feel that it is a good practice to have building principals attend and participate in all meetings of the Board of Education? Why or why not?
3. What should John do about his feuding principals?
4. Is the proposal to cut the program to hire remedial reading teachers a wise step for this district? Why or why not?

## ADDITIONAL RESOURCES

Borland, James H. *Rethinking Gifted Education.* Education and Psychology of the Gifted Series. New York: Teachers College Press, 2003.
Freeman, Joan. 2006. "Giftedness in the Long Term." *Journal for the Education of the Gifted* 29: 384–403.

National Association for the Gifted Child. 2005. *Educators*, http://www.nagc.org. (Accessed April 11, 2007)

Oakland, Thomas, and Eric Rossen. 2005. "A 21st-Century Model for Identifying Students for Gifted and Talented Programs in Light of National Conditions: An Emphasis on Race and Ethnicity." *Gifted Child Today* 28(4): 56–63.

Rayneri, Letty J., Brian L. Gerber, and Larry P. Wiley. 2006. "The Relationship between Classroom Environment and the Learning Style Preferences of Gifted Middle School Students and the Impact on Levels of Performance." *Gifted Child Quarterly* 50(2) 104–118.

Van Tassel-Baska, Joyce, and Tamra Stambaugh. 2005. "Challenges and Possibilities for Serving Gifted Learners in the Regular Classroom." *Theory Into Practice* 44: 211–217.

*Case Study 15*

# Church and State

## *freedom of religion*

"Congress shall make no law respecting an establishment of religion, or prohibiting the free exercise thereof." The legal interpretation of these words from the First Amendment of the U.S. Constitution has been a source of contention in our courts at least since the 1920s. In what was perhaps the most famous early case, a local judge upheld the right of a school board to ban the teaching of evolution, in part because Charles Darwin's book The *Origin of a Species* seemed to contain a scientific theory that was inconsistent with the explanation of creation in the Bible. Since then, the courts have overturned any restriction on teaching evolution, and today we have cases in which Christians are attempting to ensure that creationism or intelligent design is taught in schools.

Other cases involving Bible reading and prayer have also gained the attention of the courts and the American public, which remains divided on the appropriate place of religion in our public schools. There have been conflicts in many communities about religious music, prayer as a part of public ceremonies such as graduation, along with a variety of other issues related to the interpretation of the First Amendment. As our nation becomes increasingly diverse in its religious beliefs, it seems likely that it will continue to be an issue that will face our school administrators.

Sometimes high school principal, Daniel Mancuso, wished he had attended law school. It seemed that he was always calling the superintendent to ask that she get a legal opinion concerning some situation that had arisen at Northville High School. The current problem had been festering among a few students for several weeks. Now, a parent, who happened to be an attorney, had made a complaint to him that he felt could not be ignored.

The lawyer, Jeffery Larson, claimed that he was speaking for his daughter, Anne, as well as a number of other students. He claimed that the students he was representing included a member of the Jewish faith, as well as others who considered themselves either agnostics or atheists. All of the students in the group claimed to be offended by the bulletin board display of ACTIONS, the Christian group in the school. ACTIONS was an acronym for Association of Christian Teens In Our Northville Schools, which was one of the dozen school organizations that had applied for and been granted their own bulletin boards outside of the school cafeteria. In addition, each club had recently been allowed to set up its own Web site, with a link from the high school's main page. The protesting students were also unhappy with some of what was posted in the Christian organization's site.

Although the sites were a new idea, the club bulletin boards had been displayed in the hall for the past seven years. Until now, there had been no major problems with the bulletin boards. Most of the clubs used their space to post notices of upcoming meetings, minutes of past meetings, or perhaps pictures of recent events.

Dan recalled that ACTIONS had been a campus organization for at least ten years. He remembered that the legal opinion he received when the club requested to meet in school was that, even though it was not a school-sponsored organization, it could be allowed if other student groups also met in classrooms after school hours. He also had been told at the time that the group must have a faculty or staff member present at the meetings but that this person could not be the leader of the group. Matthew River had worked as the advisor of ACTIONS since its inception. In large part because of his diplomacy, there had been no significant problems in the past.

Another aspect of the current problem was that the group had recently placed a box for prayer requests in the main office. It had only been in the office for three months, and until today, there had been no major objections. Jeffery happened to see it as he was waiting to speak to Dan and questioned whether the box really belonged in a public school. The reality was, in the past week, the prayer box had become a receptacle for a hate note addressed to the club. The principal learned about this development from Melissa Erwin who was the president of ACTIONS More than any other aspect of the issue, the note upset Dan. He feared that something unpleasant might happen to the leaders of the Christian association. Personally, he was a practicing Christian who was active in the Trinity Presbyterian Church and was supportive of the club's presence in the school.

During the past several weeks, he had developed a great deal of empathy for Melissa, who he saw as a wonderful young student who was merely attempting to be a good Christian. When he turned to the Web site to review what the students had posted, he found that they had included their statement of identity which said that "ACTIONS is a group of students who believe it is possible, through Jesus, to know God and enjoy him forever." In addition, there was a verse from the New Testament that was changed regularly. The rest of the site was devoted to the names of the officers, the schedule for meetings, and dates for trips to the city mission. The visitor to the site would also be treated to music, which currently included a song by the Christian rock group, Newsboys.

Before he called the superintendent, he decided to take a walk down the hall to take a close look at the club's bulletin board. What he found was a display that read in large letters, "Jesus is King." The board was wrapped in gold paper and had a small pocket with the words "Please take one," written on it. In this pocket were slips of paper, one of which Dan pulled out to examine. On the slip was a Bible verse about the three gifts of the Magi and an explanation of each one in relation to the character of Jesus. When he finished reviewing the slip, he replaced it in the pocket and looked at the rest of the board. The explanation for this week's gift was also written out prominently on the board itself. In addition, there was a section with meeting times for the group and an invitation stating, "Any students seeking Christ are welcome to join our weekly meetings." Just before he returned to his office, he noticed that on the ACTIONS bulletin board, as well as on all the bulletin boards of the clubs, was a small disclaimer in the lower right hand corner. It said, "This board represents the views of a student led club and does not necessarily reflect the views of the school." When he sat back down at his computer, he revisited the Web site and noticed that it too had this disclaimer at the bottom.

Because he knew the superintendent would want to know his opinion, he considered the options for dealing with his church and state problem. There were two aspects of the issue that had been raised by the parent and the protesting students. First and foremost was the bulletin board. If what was posted on the bulletin board was considered illegal, it would seem likely that the messages on the Web site would also be questionable. The second issue dealt with the prayer request box. Dan felt the box didn't really hurt anyone, although if it was going to become a place to deposit hate notes, it should probably be removed.

He knew that ending the organization's privileges would satisfy the protesters and forestall any legal action by critics of the club. On the other hand, he was also certain that Melissa and her band of Christian students would not go down without a fight. They too could consider legal action based on discrimination. If they chose, they could probably find support for their cause from a number of the churches in the community. He could imagine a Board of Education meeting in the auditorium with hundreds of Christians and non-Christians there eager to express their opinions.

Perhaps there was a compromise that both groups of students could reach without involving members of the community or the courts. Dan knew that for his boss, this type of solution would be preferable. If he was going to try diplomacy, he was certain that he first had to get the opinion of the school attorney. He also knew that he would have to find a way to put aside his personal support for the club and to implement a solution that was in keeping with the current interpretation of the law regarding the relationship between church and state.

## DISCUSSION QUESTIONS

1. What is your view on the likely constitutionality of the ACTIONS bulletin board and Web site?
2. What is your view on the likely constitutionality of the prayer request box located in the school office?
3. If the school attorney does not rule against the ACTIONS group, what should Dan do about his dilemma? Should he deal with the protesting students or Jeffery Larson?

## ADDITIONAL RESOURCES

Anti Defamation League. 2004. *Religion in the Public Schools* (Student Religious Clubs). http://www.adl.org/religion_ps_2004/clubs.asp. (Accessed April 11, 2007)

Essex, Nathan L. 2006. "Student Distribution of Religious Fliers in Public Schools: Ten Ways to Invite a Lawsuit." *Clearing House: A Journal of Educational Strategies, Issues and Ideas* 79: 138–143.

Haynes, Charles C. *Religious Liberty and the Public Schools.* Bloomington, IN: Phi Delta Kappa International, 2001.

Russo, Charles J., and Ralph D. Mawdsley. 2001. "The Supreme Court Permits Religious Groups to Use Public School Facilities: Good News Club v. Milford Central School." *School Business Affairs* 67(9): 62–65.

*Case Study 16*

# Is the System Really Fair?

*discipline policies*

**Assistant principals are often required to be heavily involved in school discipline. It is not unusual for these administrators to spend much of their time dealing with students who have been referred to the office for violating school rules or being disruptive in a classroom. Many schools have attempted to make clear to the students the specific consequences for breaking school rules. Having unambiguous penalties for violations in one way simplifies the administrator's responsibility. As soon as a disciplinarian is persuaded that a student has broken one of the rules, the student handbook will prescribe the appropriate penalty. Sometimes such inflexible rules can raise the question of fairness as situations can be, and often are, quite different. In this case study, an assistant principal is troubled by several incidents that appear to need special consideration.**

Roger Lawrence had only been an assistant principal for six months, but he was already beginning to feel uncomfortable with some of the disciplinary rules and consequences listed in the Lockhaven City Middle School Student Handbook. Today's problem was the newest issue that raised questions in his mind, but there had been others. Just a few minutes ago, he had received a panicked call from Mrs. Melodee Mann, an eighth grade English teacher. She had excitedly told him that there was a fight going on in her classroom and that she had been unable to separate the two boys. Roger could hear students' voices in the background, and he knew that he needed to get to the classroom as soon as possible.

When he arrived, he found the entire class on their feet watching two boys rolling on the floor. Chairs and desks had been knocked over, and the classroom was in a state of anarchy. Roger quickly bent over and grabbed the arm of the larger boy and struggled with the other hand to hold off his opponent. With a great deal of effort, he managed to drag the student he was holding into the hall and sternly directed him to go to the waiting room outside the principal's office. When he was sure that his directions had been followed, he personally walked the other combatant to his own office waiting room and told him not to move.

With the two pugilists separated, he returned to the classroom to talk with those who had witnessed the fight. Melodee told him that it started when Arnold Clayton had come up behind Jamie Lincoln and hit him in the right shoulder while at the same time saying to him, "how are you doing today, little twerp?" Asked if she had ever seen Arnold say or do anything to Jamie prior to this incident, the teacher recalled that on several other occasions in class he had called Jamie a "twerp" and that he seemed to think that the name was funny. When he had grabbed Arnold to break up the fight, Roger noticed that he was very big for an eighth grader. It looked as though he was at least five-foot-nine and probably weighed at least 165 pounds.

Melodee also explained that Arnold was new to the school, and he had worked hard to establish himself as one of the strongest and toughest boys in the class. She suggested that he had made only a few friends and was not doing very well academically. It was her hope that when he reached high school he might gain some recognition by participating on the football or wrestling team.

Roger knew something about the other boy. Jamie was a fine student who was the son of a minister in the district. He was probably no more than five-foot-two and weighed about 120 pounds. Despite the size difference, it had appeared to the assistant principal that he was holding his own in the wrestling match on the floor. After talking with several students who had witnessed the beginning of the fight, he was able to verify their teacher's account.

On his way back to the office, he stopped at the principal's office to pick up Arnold and then escorted him directly into his own office, leaving Jamie to sit in the waiting room. He knew that he would first have to talk to the boys separately. After that, he would try to bring them together and get them to shake hands. He had learned that too often fights that began in school often would be continued off school grounds. In anticipation of his conversations, he thought it quite likely that Arnold would say that he "was just kidding around." On the other hand, Jamie would mention the fact that the Arnold had been bothering him for weeks.

Like many of the fights he had dealt with, this one had occurred because one of the students, more than the other, had been the aggressor. At least in Roger's mind, it was unfortunate that the school rules concerning fighting would require him to give both boys a two-day out-of-school suspension. Knowing without a doubt that Arnold had been the aggressor, Roger felt uncomfortable with the equal penalty required by the rule.

As he thought about the unfairness involved in this issue, it brought to mind another incident that had occurred the previous week. His administrative assistant had brought a seventh grader named Jane Hopkins into his office one morning, whom she reported had come into school late for the third time during the semester. The handbook rule concerning lateness to school stated that students would be given a one day in-school suspension after their third unexcused tardiness. When he asked Jane why she had been late three times, she told Roger that some days her mother was called to work early. When that happened, Jane had to stay home with her six-year-old brother until his school bus picked him up. When this happened, it was impossible for her to get to school on time.

Roger asked Jane why her mother didn't at least call the school office before she went to work. The student replied that her mother had tried to call the school but the line was busy. Roger could understand this as the school office phone seemed to be constantly busy during the half-hour before school opened. It was true, however, that Jane's mother had never informed the school of the situation, even later in the day. Feeling that he had no other alternative, he had assigned the girl to in-school suspension but did not feel right about it.

One additional incident had stuck in his mind. One of the math teachers, Mr. Timothy Kelly, had sent a student to the office for being disrespectful. This was another offense that carried with it one day in the in-school suspension room. After talking with the boy and the teacher, he had pieced together the exchange that led to the show of disrespect. Bobby Richards had been whispering to a student across the aisle from him and Timothy, who was known for being sarcastic with students at times, was quoted as saying, "Mr. Richards, perhaps if you listened to the teacher you might cease to be the class dunce." Bobby, who also could have a sharp tongue, said, "Yes, and if the class had a decent teacher, maybe students would listen." Timothy wasted no time in writing a referral and sending Bobby to Roger's office. The referral specifically noted the handbook policy dealing with students being disrespectful to teachers.

With this event, along with the others, Roger thought he had no choice but to send the boy to the in-school suspension room. He later spoke briefly with the teacher and suggested that calling his student a dunce was not the best idea. Although he rather meekly agreed, the boy still missed a day of classes.

What was really bothering Roger was the very specific rules and consequences that the school had adopted. Although on the surface at least, these rules made his job easier, the approach limited the disciplinarian's ability to achieve true justice. He thought about talking with Elizabeth Wheeler, the middle school principal, but he knew that she was the person who had written the handbook. He also knew that compared with many school principals, Elizabeth had the reputation of running a very tight ship.

# DISCUSSION QUESTIONS

1. Should schools develop policies that require that students receive the same penalties for a specific offense, or should administrators be given more flexibility in enforcing the disciplinary policy? Give your reasons for your position on this question.
2. If an administrator was allowed flexibility in dealing with disciplinary infractions, how would you deal with the three situations described in this case study?
3. Should Roger talk to Elizabeth about his feelings regarding the current policy? Why or why not?

# ADDITIONAL RESOURCES

Chaltain, Sam. 2006, October 25. "To Make Schools Safe, Make All Children Visible." *Education Week* 26(9): 48.

Denton, Paula. 2003. "Shared Rule-Making in Practice: The Jefferson Committee at Kingston High School." *American Secondary Education* 31: 66–97.

Gottfredson, Gary D., and Denise C. Gottfredson. 2001. "What Schools Do to Prevent Problem Behavior and Promote Safe Environments." *Journal of Educational & Psychological Consultation* 12: 313–344.

Hendly, Sarah L. 2007. "Use Positive Behavior Support for Inclusion in the General Education Classroom." *Intervention in School & Clinic* 42: 225–228. Retrieved April 10, 2007, from Professional Development Collection.

Stader, David L., and Dannie B. Francis. 2003. "Knocking at the Schoolhouse Gate." *Clearing House* 76(3): 116–119.

# What Should We Do with the Extra Money?

## *state funding*

**School districts receive most of their operating budget from state aid and local property taxes. A much smaller percentage comes from the federal government. In developing the annual school budget, administrators cannot decide on the local property tax rate until they have some idea of how much state and federal aid they will receive for the coming year. In some states, this information is not available until quite late in the budget preparation process. Sometimes when the state legislature is late in adopting a budget, local districts are forced to guess how much state aid they will receive. If state aid does not reach the estimated figures of a school district, budget cuts will have to be made. On rare occasions, a school may receive more state aid than anticipated. Such an occurrence is the subject of this case study.**

It had only happened one other time during his seventeen years as the superintendent of the Redding Hills Central School District. Last week Harold Vance was informed that his district would receive $180,000 more in state aid than he had anticipated when he began preparing the budget. It was now very late in the process and in one week he would need to present a final budget proposal to the Board of Education. At his meeting with administrators the previous week, he announced the windfall, and the session this morning was devoted to considering possibilities for using the extra funds.

During the meeting that had just concluded Harold spent most of his time listening and taking notes on the suggestions put forward by the other administrators. He thought that he would now take some time reviewing these ideas.

The first recommendation was made by the assistant superintendent for business. He recommended that $140,000 be used to reduce the property tax rate. If this was done, the district could advertise to the community that taxes were going up less than the rate of inflation. Harold had to admit that during his tenure as superintendent, the district had always raised taxes slightly higher than the inflation rate. It seemed likely that such a move would be appreciated in their community. For years the leaders of the chamber of commerce had publicly questioned why the tax rate increase always exceeded the rise in the cost of living.

The fact that the additional $180,000 in state aid was now public knowledge would undoubtedly cause taxpayers to wonder why the funds were not used to reduce the taxes. The assistant superintendent also argued that the decision would be welcomed by the growing number of senior citizens in the community. Many of these people were on fixed incomes, and some of them were having difficulties keeping up with the escalating property taxes.

In addition to the reduction in taxes, the business official recommended that $40,000 be added to the small reserve fund that the district was legally able to maintain. Even with this addition to the fund, which could be used for any emergency expenditure, the district would still be below the amount allowed for such a fund by the state regulations. Although this recommendation certainly needed to be considered, the administrators who were responsible for the academic programs had different ideas as to how the money should be used.

One of the elementary principals had made the suggestion that the money be used to establish a preschool classroom in each of the district's elementary schools. Because the elementary enrollment had been declining, there was at least one unused classroom in each of the schools. This administrator pointed to the nationwide trend that was causing an increasing number of public schools to establish preschool programs in their buildings. He cited Georgia that already had classes involving "more than sixty-one thousand four-year-olds" in their public schools.[1]

In support of his recommendation, the principal claimed that research had proven that quality preschool programs will cause children to perform "better on measures of both cognitive skills (for example, math and language abilities) and social skills (for example, interactions with peers, problem behaviors)."[2] The administrator was sure that with the money that was available, the district could not only pay three preschool education teachers, but could also purchase the necessary equipment and supplies for the three classrooms. Pointing to the success of the Head Start programs around the country, he was convinced that these classes would have a positive influence on the future test scores in the district.

Another elementary principal, although she agreed that preschool education was important, raised several questions about her colleagues' proposal. She wondered out loud which four-year-olds would be given the privilege of participating in the program. She also pointed out that some of the children, especially if they were determined to be in need of special education, might need additional services. If they did, would it mean that they would have to hire more speech therapists, occupational therapists, or physical therapists? As far as test scores were concerned, she believed that she had an idea that would bring improved results even sooner than preschool programs.

She began her proposal by noting that next year there would be approximately 240 first graders in the district. The average class size was slated to be twenty students. If they hired an additional first grade teacher in each of the elementary schools, the class size could be cut to sixteen. This administrator had also come to the meeting with research that showed that class size reductions in kindergarten through third grade can have a long-term influence on the success of students.

Among others, she pointed to the Star Study in the state of Tennessee. This was a large, long-term project that was generally accepted in the education community to have shown a very positive influence of smaller classes at the primary level. She quoted a statement that appeared in a book by Timothy A. Hacsi. The book suggested that students who had been educated in smaller classes did better on a variety of standardized tests, were less likely to drop out of school, more likely to graduate from high school on time, more likely to take advanced courses, earn high grades, and go to college. [3] The principal also pointed out that first grade was where students really began to read and do math and, as far as she was concerned, it was the first place to begin a reduction in class size. It was her hope that in future years, similar cuts in class size could be made in the other primary grades.

The principals of the middle school and high school also had their own plan. They saw the extra money as a wonderful opportunity to improve the technology available to the teachers and students in their buildings. In particular, they were anxious to begin the upgrade in the math and science classrooms in grades seven through twelve. Their argument included the observation that a technology initiative would be well-received by the Board of Education and the community. They pointed to the fact that several years ago there had been a bond issue vote to allow the district to borrow money to put computers in every classroom. That proposition had been approved by the voters by a two to one margin. Supporters of the referendum had successfully argued that it was absolutely necessary for the school to enter the computer age.

The two administrators had prepared a joint proposal. They wanted to purchase sixty classroom technology units, which included a computer with Microsoft Office, a pull-down screen, and a projector. This equipment would allow teachers and students to play DVDs, show PowerPoint presentations, and do in-class research. The cost would be approximately $3,000 for each unit.

After reading through his notes on the four suggestions made by the administrative team, Harold wished there was enough money to do all of them.

Of course there also might be some ideas that had yet to be considered. He also knew that it was possible to compromise and divide the money between two or more of the plans although doing so might well reduce the overall impact of the expenditures. The practical side of him agreed with the business administrator, but he expected that this might be the last time in his career he would have extra money available. Given the opportunity, he really wanted to find a way to improve the academic program in his school.

## DISCUSSION QUESTIONS

1. Identify one additional way the school district might use these funds. Give your rationale for the suggestion.
2. Discuss one possible problem that might arise with each of the options of the administrative team.
3. If you were superintendent, what would you recommend to the Board of Education as the best way to use these extra funds? Give the reasons for your recommendation.

## NOTES

1. Diana Early, Dick Clifford, and Tynnette Hills, "Public Schools and Pre-K Services," *NCEDL Research*, http://www.fpg.unc.edu/~ncedl/pages/project_summary studyid=25. (Accessed March 8, 2007)

2. Ellen Peisner-Feinberg, Richard Clifford, Peg Burchinal, Noreen Yazejian, Patty Byler, and Jean Rustici, "The Children of the Cost, Quality & Outcomes Study Go to School," *NCEDL Research*, http://www.fpg.unc.edu/~ncedl/pages/project_summary .cfm?studyid=7 (8 March 2007).

3. Timothy A. Hacsi, *Children as Pawns*, (Cambridge, MA: Harvard University Press, 2003), 119–120.

## ADDITIONAL RESOURCES

Anderson, Bill. 1980. "This, Too, Is Trouble: A Budget with a $40 Million Surplus." *American School Board Journal* 167(10): 26–28, 40.

Fletcher, Geoffrey. H. 2005. "Why Aren't Dollars Following Need? The Need for Professional Development is Enormous and Expressed; The Question Is, Where's the Money?" *T.H.E. Journal* 32(11): 4.

Goldberg, Kalman. 2000. "School Finance Reform in a Growing Economy: Using the Growth Dividend." *Journal of Education Finance* 25: 433–456.

Muir, Mike, Gerald Knezek, and Rhonda Christensen. 2004. "The Power of One to One: Early Finding from the Maine Learning Technology Initiative." *Learning & Leading with Technology* 32(3): 6–11.

Pruslow, John T. 2001. "What Do We Spend to Educate a Child? The Student Resource Allocation Model." *School Business Affairs* 67(11): 33–36.

Schweke, William. 2006. "Smart Money: Public Investment in Public Education." *School Administrator* 63(2). Retrieved April 19, 2007, from Professional Development Collection.

*Case Study 18*

# Military Recruiters in Schools

*students' right to privacy*

**During the last half century, public schools, on a number of occasions, have become involved in national political conflicts. Beginning with the case of *Brown v. The Board of Education of Topeka Kansas* in 1954, public schools became a battleground for the struggle for civil rights. Following this decision, which eventually brought an end to publicly sanctioned separate schools for whites and nonwhites, many districts chose or were forced to introduce busing programs to end de facto segregation in metropolitan school districts throughout the country. These court-sanctioned mandates, along with other affirmative action programs that attempted to promote diversity in hiring school personnel, had a major impact in a number of school districts. The 1972 law popularly known as Title IX also was in large part a way to ensure equal opportunity for girls in our schools.**

**Certainly cases involving the interpretation of the first amendment restrictions on the federal government's role in the area of religion and freedom of speech have been major issues in our schools. During the late 1960s and early 1970s, high school students also became involved in protests against the Vietnam War. The nation is now engaged in another unpopular war that is causing a stir in a number of high schools.**

When she saw the envelope that noted that the enclosed letter was from the American Civil Liberties Union, veteran high school principal, Catherine Weaver made the quick assumption that she probably had a new problem. She was quite familiar with the organization. Upon opening it, she noticed that it had been sent to a number of school administrators and that it was signed by the executive director of the organization along with two staff attorneys. The letter read as follows:

To: All Principals, Albany County High Schools, Columbia County High Schools, Greene County High Schools, Rensselaer County High Schools,

Saratoga County High Schools, Schenectady County High Schools, Warren County High Schools and Washington County High Schools

Re: Military Recruitment of Your Students

We understand that over the summer you may have received a letter from a local Department of the Army official demanding that you provide the military with information about current and past students of yours. That letter, a copy of which we enclose, contains many inaccuracies and calls for actions on your part that would violate student privacy rights.

We therefore write to provide you with accurate information about your obligations when it comes to military recruiting and to inform you of various options available to you and your staff to protect the privacy interests of your students. We also are available to answer questions or to provide you with additional assistance.

As you presumably know, two recently enacted federal statutes do require school districts to take certain actions with respect to efforts by the United States military to recruit high school students. (Those statutes are the "No Child Left Behind Act" ("NCLB"), and the "National Defense Authorization Act for Fiscal Year 2002" ("NDAA"). Unfortunately, the letter you received from Commanding Officer Lawrence Mullany misstates the obligations imposed on school officials by these statutes in a number of important respects:

1. *Schools Cannot Release Any Information Before Offering Students and Families the Opportunity to Object.* The Army letter directs schools to release student information before notifying parents and students of their rights to object. Instead, the letter promises to purge the names of those students who have objected after the fact. [paragraphs 3 and 4]. This directive violates both NCLB and NDAA.

Prior to any disclosure of directory information under NCLB and NDAA, a school must advise students and their parents that they may object to the disclosure of directory information without written parental consent and the school may not release student directory information if the student or parent objects.

2. *Schools Cannot Release Information about Former Students.* The Army letter directs schools to release information pertaining to former students [paragraph 1]. NCLB and NDAA do not authorize the release of directory information except with respect to those students who are currently enrolled in your high school.

3. *Schools Cannot Release Information about Any Student Who Is Not a Senior or Junior.* The Army letter directs recipient schools to provide information pertaining to all students, regardless of age or grade level [paragraph 1]. The U.S. Department of Education and the U.S. Department of Defense have restricted NCLB and NDAA military recruiter access to information concerning only

those students who are seventeen years of age or older or are in the eleventh grade or higher.

4. *Schools Cannot Release Students E-mail Addresses, Ages or Birthdates.* The Army letter directs recipient schools to provide this information as well as student e-mail addresses, ages or dates of birth, and class levels [paragraph 1]. NCLB and NDAA permit military recruiter access only to "student names, addresses and telephone numbers."

5. *Schools Are Not Required by the Statutes to Employ an "Opt-Out" Procedure.* The Army letter states that NCLB and NDAA prohibit schools from establishing an "opt-in" procedure for disclosure [paragraph 2]. While it is true that these statutes direct schools to comply with a request for student directory information, they are silent as to how a school must comply.

The New York Civil Liberties Union urges you to protect the privacy of your students by setting up user-friendly procedures that notify students and their families of their rights under NCLB and NDAA and makes it easy for them to control the disclosure of their student directory information.

Finally, though NCLB and NDAA require schools to give military recruiters the same campus access that is offered to representatives of higher education and prospective employers, schools are not required to give preferential treatment to military recruiters. For example, schools that require a forum for students to hear alternative views on controversial issues should apply the rule to military representatives. Schools that exclude employers that practice discrimination, should also apply that policy to the military, which engages in discrimination based on sexual orientation. The New York Court of Appeals has upheld the right of public schools in New York to apply nondiscrimination policies to the military.

Sincerely,

Donna Lieberman
Executive Director

Beth Haroules
Alan Silver
Staff Attorneys[1]

Catherine was confused by some aspects of the letter and was not sure that she should accept the legal interpretations of the American Civil Liberties Union. That afternoon she was even more perplexed on reading an article in *USA Today*. It carried the headline, "War Opponents Target Military Recruiters in High Schools." She had reread the first paragraph several times. It went as follows:

High schools are the latest antiwar battleground with parents, students, educators, and activists around the country stepping up campaigns to prevent military recruiters from reaching students. Many of the efforts focus on a provision in President Bush's 2002 No Child Left Behind law that requires federally funded secondary schools to give military recruiters the same access to students as they do college or job recruiters.[2]

The article continued on about "opt-out" alternatives that had been mentioned in the letter she had received. It explained that:

> "Opt-out" events planned through November in 321 communities are giving parents and students 18 or older forms asking school officials to not release personal information or school records to military officials. They can send similar requests to the Pentagon. By Tuesday, more than 24,000 opt-outs had been requested, says Leave My Child Alone, a national coalition coordinating the events. Meanwhile, a bill introduced by U.S. Rep. Mike Honda, D-Calif., would prevent schools from releasing private information to military recruiters unless families request it.[3]

Later in the story was an account of recent events in Seattle where the Board of Education "voted to tighten districtwide military recruitment policies and make clear that conscientious objectors can have equal access to students." Parents in Toledo, Ohio, received in the mail a brochure from the school district highlighting the "opt-out" option. Numerous local and national groups have been formed to limit the ability of the military to recruit high school students. A spokesman for one of these groups is quoted as saying that, "the antirecruitment drive is the next big thing for the antiwar movement."[4] For others it isn't so much an antiwar movement, but rather a privacy issue.

Although Catherine expected that there would be a number of individuals in her affluent suburban school district who would support an antirecruitment stand by the high school, she knew that there would be others, including possibly veterans groups, who would balk at any attempt to curtail military recruitment. Personally, on several occasions, she had conversations with military recruiters who were visiting the school. They were always polite and respectful to her and to other faculty and staff. They were very much like the college recruiters who visited the school guidance office. On the other hand, she had no idea what they were saying to the students, nor had she ever looked at the literature they were distributing.

Catherine decided to go on the Internet to see if she could gather any additional information. The first article she found was a story in the *Christian Science Monitor*. The article pointed out that the Supreme Court had recently accepted a case to decide whether the federal government could withhold funds from colleges that barred military recruiters. This article suggested that, "nationally, there's a growing sense that recruiters desperate to bolster falling enlistment numbers are misrepresenting sign-up agreements to entice recruits. In response to 480 allegations of improprieties by recruiters since Oct. 1, the Army announced it will suspend its recruiting for one day on May 20, so commanders can remind its 7,500 recruiters of proper conduct."[5]

The more she read the less certain she became about whether her students were being subjected to inappropriate tactics by the visiting military recruiters. Catherine had to admit that she really didn't know what was happening in this area. She was quite certain, however, that if she began to raise questions, it could create an issue that would only get larger. Her feelings about the matter were also influenced by the fact that she had become a strong critic of the war in Iraq.

One of the events that had solidified her antiwar feelings was the recent death of one of her school's graduates. Charles Webb had been a very patriotic young man who had decided to put off college to serve his country. He had been in Iraq for just three weeks when he became a victim of a suicide bomber. As she thought about the tragedy of Charles' death, it occurred to Catherine that he might well have been convinced to join the army by a recruiter in her school.

She put this disturbing thought aside and placed the letter in the top drawer of her desk. The safest course of action seemed to be to ignore the issue or to at least wait until someone formally complained about the military recruiters. Knowing herself well, she was aware that she would be uneasy about the decision to do nothing. Before leaving for home that day, she reread the letter from the Civil Liberties Union for the third time.

## DISCUSSION QUESTIONS

1. Do you support the provision in the No Child Left Behind Act that requires that schools must allow military recruiters in their building? Why or why not?
2. Should Catherine allow her personal convictions concerning the war to affect any decision she makes as a school administrator?
3. If you were principal of a high school, what if anything would you do about the letter from the Civil Liberties Union? If your answer is that you would do nothing, give your reasons. If you were to act on the letter, what would you do?

## NOTES

1. Donna Lieberman, "Letter from the ACLU to NY Public High School Principals About the No Child Left Behind Act," *ACLU*, September 22, 2003, http://www.aclu .org/privacy/youth/15652res20030922.html. (Accessed March 7, 2007)

2. Mary Beth Marklein, "War Opponents Target Military Recruiters in High Schools," *USA Today*, September 20, 2005, http://www.usatoday.com/news/nation/2005-09-20-war-opponents-schools_x.htm. (Accessed March 19, 2007)

3. Marklein, "War Opponents Target Military Recruiters in High Schools," 1.

4. Marklein, "War Opponents Target Military Recruiters in High Schools," 1.

5. Dean Paton, "Rift over recruiting at public high schools," *Christian Science Monitor*, May 18, 2005, http://www.csmonitor.com/2005/0518/p02s01-ussc.html. (Accessed March 19, 2007)

## ADDITIONAL RESOURCES

Ayers, William. 2006. "Military Recruiters Are Using and Abusing Our Kids." *Phi Delta Kappan* 8: 594–299.

Christine, Charles T. 2006. "Not the Military I Know." *Phi Delta Kappan* 88: 253–257.

Gewertz, C. 2007. "Defense Dept. Settles Suit on Student-Recruiting Database." *Education Week* 26(19): 7. Goodman, David. 2003. "Covertly Recruiting Kids." *AlterNet* http://www.alternet.org/story/16856/. (Accessed April 21, 2007)

Hardy, Lawrence. 2005. "A Girl Sues the Military Over recruiter tricks." *American School Board Journal* 192: 26–29.

Merrow, John. 2004. "High School Recruiting: A Look Inside the Army's Recruiting Efforts on High School Campuses." In *Merrow Report*. http://www.pbs.org/merrow/tv/newshour/recruit.html. (Accessed April 21, 2007)

*Case Study 19*

# Closing a School

*restructuring a district*

**In sections of the country where public school enrollments are declining, school district officials often face the necessity of closing schools. Such decisions are most often a problem of larger urban districts, but sometimes even smaller communities have to consider closing schools. As administrators approach such decisions, there are a number of factors that will affect any decision. In any case, closing one or more schools can become controversial and sometimes painful for a community. Prior to moving forward on such an action, school district officials must do their homework carefully as they may well face organized opposition to their decision.**

The city of Oakridge had a population of approximately twenty-three thousand people in 1960. When the most recent census was published, that number had declined to less than nineteen thousand, and city officials expected that there would be additional losses reported in the next census. As superintendent of the Oakridge City Schools, Dr. Brian Tucker was familiar with the causes of the decline in population. Much of it was due to the loss of a major automotive assembly plant that at one time had employed close to five thousand workers. The closure of the factory had been a tremendous blow to the economy of the city. One could easily observe boarded-up buildings that had once housed successful businesses.

With the reduction of the business tax base came a similar decline in residential assessments as the real estate market experienced a severe decline. For the past several years, on driving through the city, one could not help but notice the many "For Sale" signs in front of homes. The economic conditions in the community also had an effect on the student population. It was not only that young parents were leaving the city to find new work, but there were many who had good jobs who decided to seek homes in the suburbs. As a result, the city population was increasingly made up of older residents, and in several sections, racial and ethnic minorities had become the majority.

Another event that had a dramatic impact on the elementary enrollment was the opening of the city's first charter school last year. Located in the former office building of the automobile plant, the school enrolled one hundred and fifty students in kindergarten through sixth grade. Because it had received more than two hundred applications, it seemed likely that if the school succeeded, it would expand in the near future.

As a result of the reduction in students, the six elementary buildings all had a significant number of empty classrooms. For the past three years, the district had not replaced teachers who had retired and even chose not to fill other vacancies that occurred. At its peak, the elementary schools had close to two hundred and fifty teachers and other professional support personnel, but because of the loss of students, that number had declined to slightly fewer than two hundred. The number of empty classrooms in the schools ranged from three to seven, and the total number for the district was thirty-five. There was no question that five buildings would accommodate the current elementary population, and there was little reason to believe that the numbers would grow in the near future. This was not the only problem facing the district. Five of the buildings were at least forty years old with two of them having been built more than sixty years ago. Although all of them were safe, there were serious maintenance issues that the district had been forced to ignore.

Because of his concern about the need to close a building, Brian had been reading about problems caused when districts attempted to introduce school closing plans. In Detroit, the teacher's union had led the opposition; in Seattle, it had been parents of minority children who had stalled the closure program. The problem was different in Washington, DC, where the enrollment decline had been caused by the fact that twenty-six percent of the city's children were attending charter schools.[1] The only consolidations that seemed to go smoothly were those that occurred when a new building was constructed, and parents were enthusiastic about having their children benefit from a modern facility. There would be no new facility in Oakridge.

Realizing that it would be irresponsible to ignore the issue any longer, Brian had raised the issue at his last administrative meeting. Along with the assistant superintendents and principals, he invited the superintendent of buildings and grounds and the transportation director. The discussion during the meeting raised numerous issues but had not identified which of the six schools should be closed.

The superintendent of buildings and grounds reported on the future maintenance projects that had to be considered at each of the buildings. There was no question that the sixty-year-old Frederick Douglas Elementary School had the largest number of issues that needed to be addressed in the near future. These projects included a new roof and heating system. The current boilers were extremely inefficient and required frequent repair. As they talked about the building, the assistant superintendent for instruction mentioned the high degree of loyalty of the students and parents to this neighborhood school. Many of the children were third generation students in the building. He also pointed out that the African American families, which made up three-quarters of the school population, might not be happy with the decision to close their school.

The assistant superintendent for instruction believed there might be a more important factor in choosing a school to close. Although the test scores at Frederick Douglas were near the bottom in the district, academically the John Kennedy Elementary School had by far the worst scores in the city. There were several possible explanations for the high number of failures. Certainly, the school had some unique academic problems that were not easy to solve, and it might be good to close the building and send the teachers and students to more successful schools. On hearing this suggestion the superintendent of buildings and grounds shook his head and said that John Kennedy was their newest building and that it had the fewest maintenance problems.

The conversation then turned to the East Avenue Elementary School. Located in the corner of the district, which had lost the most population, the building had more empty classrooms than any of the other schools. The possibility of closing this facility caused the transportation director to observe that most of the kids who went to this school were able to walk from their homes. If they were to be assigned to schools throughout the city, he would have to transport them. This would require some new buses and drivers.

The assistant superintendent for business joined in the conversation by admitting that the consolidation of schools would create some additional costs, but he argued that they would be far outweighed by the savings. He estimated that closing a school would allow the district to eliminate a number of smaller classes, some of which had dipped below seventeen students. By raising average class sizes in the elementary school by no more than two students per class, he believed that five elementary school teaching positions could be eliminated. It would also be possible to have one less school librarian and one less nurse. In all likelihood, they could also reduce the number of office personnel, custodians, and cafeteria personnel. In addition, there was the fact that one of the principals was scheduled to retire and having five principals rather than six would save the district more than one hundred thousand dollars.

He went on to list likely savings in heating fuel, electricity, and other maintenance costs. Depending on which building was closed, they might also be lucky in selling it for a good price. There was no question in the mind of the business official that closing a school would help the district financially. As he considered the savings, all that Brian could think about was the impact on employees and their families who might lose their jobs. For him, the worst part of being the superintendent in Oakridge had been the annual cuts in personnel that had been necessary.

Thinking about the impact of any decision to close a school, he had asked the group whether they thought that there would be neighborhood opposition to any decision that was made. Most of the participants at the meeting agreed that schools were important to their neighborhoods and that parents who had children who could walk to school might be unhappy to hear that they had to ride a bus across the city into a strange neighborhood. An even bigger potential problem would be the assignment of additional students to Glencliff Elementary School. This school was located in the most prosperous section of the city and had by far the best academic reputation and the highest test scores. If students had to be bused to a school other than one in their neighborhood, it was likely that many families would choose Glencliff. Unfortunately, the school had only three empty classrooms. He hoped that the parents at this school would not object to an influx of new students.

On the other hand, if Frederick Douglas remained open, there might be some white parents from the well-to-do section who would object to having their children assigned to a school with seventy-five percent minorities. It was also possible that if four hundred African American students were divided among the five schools, that it would be a positive move in bringing about an integration that Brian thought was healthy. Although additional integration might be considered a positive result, there was also the possibility that it would lead to even more "white flight" to the suburbs.

One additional worry was in the back of his mind. He had heard at a recent Rotary Club meeting that a private company was preparing an application for a second charter school in the city. Was it possible that he would go through the agony of closing a school in the coming year and then have to consider another closing in the near future? In any case, he knew that he had to decide how he was going to handle the current problem. Brian would have to start by laying out the facts to the Board of Education. There was little question that this group would instruct him to move forward in preparing a plan.

## DISCUSSION QUESTIONS

1. Should Brian go to the Board of Education with a complete plan for closing a specific school or should he seek suggestions from people other than his administrative staff? Give the reasons for your answer.

2. Assume that the decision has been made to enlist others in preparing a school closing plan, what groups or individuals should be asked to participate? Give your reasons for identifying these groups or individuals.

3. What are the primary factors that you would consider in making the decision on which of Oakridge's six schools to close?

## NOTE

1. Theola Labbe, "School System Loses Students; Charters Gain," *Washington Post*, February 1, 2007 http://www.washingtonpost.com/wp-dyn/content/article/2007/01/31/AR2007013102643.html. (Accessed February 21, 2007)

## ADDITIONAL RESOURCES

Egelund, Niels, and Helen Laustsen. 2006. "School Closure: What Are the Consequences for the Local Society?" *Scandinavian Journal of Educational Research* 50: 429–439.

Hess, Frederick M. 2001."Whaddya Mean You Want to Close My School? The Politics of Regulatory Accountability in Charter Schooling." *Education and Urban Society* 33: 141–157.

McLean, Russ. 2003. "Seven Red Herrings: The Opposition to Closure of Aging Urban Schools." *Clearing House* 76: 140–142.

Tonn, Jessica L. 2007. "Savings from School Consolidation Plans Uncertain." *Education Week* 26(29): 10.

*Case Study 20*

# A School Dress Code

## *student dress*

The appropriate clothing and appearance considered acceptable for public school students has been a controversial issue for at least the last half century. One expects that it has actually been a source of concern since the beginning of the public school movement in the middle of the nineteenth century. Perhaps the single most influential event in defining the problem occurred in 1969 with the Supreme Court case *Tinker v. Des Moines Independent Community School District*. The case involved a group of students who wore black armbands to school to protest the war in Vietnam. The court ruled that their right to do so was protected as long as what they did was not disruptive.

Following this case, there have been many disputes over appearance, some of which have gone to court. The issues have included hair length for boys and the right of girls to wear pants in school rather than skirts and dresses. In 1987, students attending a senior prom in Ohio sued for the right to attend the dance dressed as a person of the opposite sex. They lost the case when the court said, "schools have the authority to enforce dress regulations that teach community values and promote school discipline." There have also been a number of cases brought about by a school's attempt to enforce rules that sought to control gang activity. Here again the court ruled in favor of the school, saying that, "the school's goal, control of youth gangs, justified any constitutional infringement."[1]

More recently, there have been a variety of decisions dealing with words on T-shirts. One federal judge upheld a student's right to wear a shirt advertising an alcoholic beverage. In another case, schools were given the right to prohibit clothes with "lewd or vulgar messages." The right of boys to wear earrings and sagging pants has also been challenged. Revealing clothing worn by young women is also an ongoing problem in our schools.[2]

Because there will always be something new in student fashions that will upset individuals in a school or community, the issue of student dress is one that will continue to confront school administrators. Discussions involving

**dress codes or even school uniforms will be ongoing, and school principals will continue to be responsible for enforcing any rules that are adopted by their district.**

After attempting to deal with the issue for over a decade, high school principal, Lou Westgate, had concluded that it might be helpful to have a more definitive school dress code. As a result, he set into motion a process that might produce such a code, but he was beginning to wish that he had never raised the issue. Currently, the student handbook at Woodrow Wilson Senior High School merely said that students were not to "wear in the building clothing that was disruptive or distracting." What Lou had found was that the members of the faculty who made most of the referrals dealing with inappropriate clothing, had standards that varied greatly. He had three or four teachers who made the majority of the complaints about student clothing, while most of the faculty never referred a student.

When he personally observed clothing he thought was a violation of the policy or a teacher made a referral, it was up to him to enforce the rule. Throughout the years he had done a number of things when he thought a student was dressed inappropriately. If a student had other clothing in school, he would merely have the student change. Often this was not an alternative and as a result, he had purchased a couple of sweatshirts from the school store and made them available to the offending students. On several occasions, the young people had balked at changing their clothes, and he was forced to call the parents and ask them to bring in some other clothing or to take their child home.

Parents were not happy about being called. One father, who had to leave work to pick up his daughter, had asked Lou if, "he had nothing better to do than to worry about a student's neckline." Although he had never been threatened with a lawsuit over any of his dress code decisions, he had upset students, parents, and teachers with his actions concerning appropriate dress.

It was for this reason that he became interested in more specific guidelines and a policy that would guide him in making decisions. To develop such a policy, he decided to establish an advisory committee. To ensure that the group represented a variety of viewpoints, he believed it was important that the committee include students, parents, and teachers. To ensure fairness, it was his plan to have three representatives from each of these groups. To lead the committee, he thought that the school's social studies department chairperson would be perfect. As the instructor of the senior American government class and a former president of the teachers' union, he knew that Mary Chaplin was an informed and affective leader. When he asked her whether she would take the job, she eagerly accepted it as a "real challenge."

At the next faculty meeting, he asked for volunteers to serve on the group. He was not surprised that the first one to raise his hand was George Linden. A sixty-two-year-old bachelor and a veteran member of the math department, George had made more referrals for improper dress than any other member of the faculty. He also had reported numerous couples for being "inappropriately affectionate" in the school hall. Lou could only image the dress code that George might wish to develop. Along with Mary and George, the other individual who raised her hand was also an older member of the faculty. She was the last member in what was once an active home economics department. Both of those teachers who volunteered might, in Lou's mind, favor a very restricted policy.

Even before he sought parents and students, Lou could not help but worry about the makeup of his committee, but it was too late to turn back. He decided that he would attend the next meeting of the Parent–Teacher Association to seek out his three parents. There were less than thirty parents present at the meeting, and when the president of the PTA explained the mission of the advisory committee and asked for volunteers, only three hands went up. Two of the individuals were sitting next to each other, and Lou learned later that they were friends who were both active in the small but vocal Conservative Party in the community. The third volunteer was an older woman who was actually a grandmother and had custody of her teenage granddaughter. When her daughter's marriage had broken up, she had taken Kelly to live with her. It had not been easy on the girl, and at age thirteen, she was already something of a discipline problem. Her grandmother was trying her best to cope; one of the constant issues was Kelly's clothing.

In considering the parent representatives on the committee, Lou was quite certain that he had gotten three individuals who might also support a very strict code. His final hope was the student volunteers, and for these committee members, he attended the student council meeting. Of the three young people who showed interest in serving, he was sure that at least two would give some balance to the committee. Mary described Lance Pearson as a "future politician." He was a member of the senior class and treasurer of the council. His social studies teacher saw him as a born diplomat, who would try hard to reach a consensus that would hopefully satisfy everyone involved. Susie Kellogg was a popular cheerleader who was very conscious of her clothing. The outfits that she wore to school were stylish and expensive, and she might well end up as the most liberal member of the committee.

The final student who volunteered was something of a mystery. She was a junior but it was her first year at the high school because she had been home-schooled up to that point. All of her teachers reported that Ester Morton was extremely intelligent and very mature for her age. Unlike Susie, her clothing might be described as quite austere.

With the selection process completed, the topic that was raised at the first meeting of the group was a surprise. When Mary came in the next day to report on the meeting, she told Lou that the group had spent the entire session debating the possibility of requiring school uniforms. The conversation had been spirited with the three parents and George supporting the idea. Following the two-hour discussion, a formal vote was taken and, by a five to four margin, the group decided that they would not recommend school uniforms.

The second session was equally lively. The three parents met outside of school to prepare a recommendation on a dress code. In reality, they had found one to their liking on the Internet. Mary, Lance, and Susie thought that many of the rules were ridiculous, however, and they argued vigorously against it. During this debate, Ester just listened quietly. George, on the other hand, was supportive of the code that was introduced by the parents. Mary told Lou that she had been sure that there were four certain votes for recommending this policy. To settle the issue, the committee agreed on a secret ballot. When the votes were counted, it showed that there were six votes in favor of the proposed dress code.

As a result, after just two meetings, Lou had on his desk what was, in reality, a copy of the secondary dress code of the Houston County Schools. It read:

### Secondary Dress Code Policy (Grades 6–12)

Goal: Students of the Houston County School System are expected to dress in a manner that is supportive of a positive learning environment that is free of distractions and disruptions. There is a direct correlation between student dress and student behavior. Students will be expected to observe modes of dress, styles of hair, and personal grooming, which support the learning environment. The purpose of this dress code is to assure that consistency and interpretation is implemented countywide, thus providing equitable treatment for all students.

### General Rules

Outer clothing which resembles loungewear, pajamas, or underwear is prohibited. Fads and styles in dress which differ extremely from conventionally accepted standards are prohibited.

Any clothing that is viewed as distracting because of extremes in style, fit, color, pattern, fabric, etc., shall not be permitted. Undergarments may not be exposed at any time.

### Specific Rules

Blouses/shirts should be constructed so that the top of the shoulder is covered and is fitted under the arms (no halter tops, tank tops, strapless tops, spaghetti straps, or bare-shouldered tops of any type will be allowed). Blouses/shirts which expose any portion of the waist, hips, or midriff are not allowed. Blouses/shirts which are not appropriate for school include those which are low-cut, see-through, backless, or tube tops.

Clothing which is cut, slashed, or has holes is prohibited.

In accordance with board policy governing student conduct with regard to bullying, weapons, gangs, and drugs: clothing shall be free of inflammatory, suggestive, racial, or other inappropriate writing, advertisement, or artwork. This includes offensive words and designs, violence (blood, death, weapons), sex, playboy symbols, hate groups, tobacco products, drugs, and alcohol.

No clothing or other article may be worn or displayed which may indicate membership in a gang at school or any school function.

Pants, skirts, and dresses must be knee-length or longer, and must have a hem. Shirts must be tucked in.

Nylon windsuits that fit appropriately are permitted.

Mesh, nylon, or athletic shorts are not permitted in the classroom. These type shorts may be worn during P.E. classes only.

### Accessories

Shoes/sandals must be worn at all times. Cleated shoes are prohibited inside the building. House/bedroom slippers are not acceptable.

Male students may not wear earrings; female students may wear earrings. Neither male nor female students may wear ornaments (jewelry) which pierce the skin such as the nose, lips, tongue, eyelid, etc.

Students may not wear hats, caps, bandanas, sunglasses, combs, picks, etc., inside the building.

### Hair & Grooming

Hair must be well-groomed. Only conventional hair coloring will be permitted. Extreme hairstyles and fads that would interfere with the learning process, cause a disruption of the educational environment, or be a health or safety hazard are prohibited.

Well-groomed mustaches are permitted; goatees and beards are prohibited.

### Coats

Due to variances in physical design of schools, principal's discretion will apply to wearing of outer garments, coats, and jackets. Students may wear coats/winter garments to school, but may be asked to store them in their lockers during the school day. Students are encouraged to bring lightweight jackets to wear in the building as changes in weather dictate.

NOTE: *Principal discretion applies to all of the above.*[3]

After his second reading of the recommendation, he was certain that it would raise havoc in both the school and in the community. If he had enforcement problems now, they would likely become even more onerous with such a policy. At the same time, he realized that this was his committee, and that they had democratically arrived at the report. The question now was, what should he do with it?

One alternative was to attempt to amend it so that it would be more manageable. If he did this, Lou was concerned that those who had voted for the plan might well have trouble accepting his changes. He knew that at some point, the Board of Education would have to approve of it, but he wanted to be comfortable with any dress code before it went to the board. Another possibility would be to share the recommendation with the three groups that had been represented on the committee. He could just imagine a student council or faculty meeting debate on the policy. For that matter, it might create a rather interesting PTA meeting as well. There were perhaps additional ways to react to the report, but he could not come up with any other possibilities. On the other hand, Lou knew that he had to do something.

## DISCUSSION QUESTIONS

1. Was the principal's idea of setting up a committee the way he did a good plan for establishing a new dress code policy? Why or why not?
2. Would you prefer to have a dress code that is general in nature or would you rather have one which attempts to define more specifically what is and is not appropriate dress? Give the reasons for your answer.
3. What should Lou do with the report?

## NOTES

1. Richard Fossey and Todd A. DeMitchell, "Litigating School Dress Codes," *Education Week*, March 19, 1997, http://www.teachermag.com/ew/vol-16/25fossey.h16. (Accessed March 21, 2007)

2. Fossey and DeMitchell, "Litigating School Dress Codes."

3. Houston County Board of Education, *Houston County Schools Secondary Dress Cody Policy*, http://www.hcbe.net/dresscode.html.

## ADDITIONAL RESOURCES

Barlow, Dudley. 2004. "The Fashion Police: Never Out of Fashion." *Education Digest: Essential Readings Condensed for Quick Review* 69(8): 64–67. Retrieved April 20, 2007, from Academic Search Premier.

Brunsma, David L. 2005. *Uniforms in Public Schools: A Decade of Research and Debate.* Lanham, MD: Rowman & Littlefield Education.

Brunsma, David L. 2004. *The School Uniform Movement and What It Tells Us about American Education: A Symbolic Crusade.* Lanham, MD: Rowman & Littlefield Education.

## Case Study 21

# What to Do about Cell Phones?

## cell phone use in schools

The introduction of new technology in schools can create problems for school administrators. Certainly, computers have raised censorship issues in recent years. There has been a need for purchasing some type of filter to monitor the sites that students could use. Many have reported that these programs are less than foolproof. In the case of cell phones, schools are still grappling with an effective way to deal with them. As early as the late 1980s, many urban schools prohibited cell phones and pagers because of the association of the devices with drug dealers. Some states also passed laws totally banning cell phones from schools. Other states and school districts have been much slower to develop a definitive policy. The events of September 11th and of the student violence at Columbine seem to have provided new justification for students to have such devices in school. Many parents appreciate the possibility of instant communication between themselves and their children, but the issue has become more complicated in recent years with the addition of new features to the phones.

It was his fourth referral this month, and there still was a week to go. Sean Kelly, the assistant principal of the Plainfield Middle School, was beginning to see a need to do something more about cell phone interruptions during classes. At an assembly at the beginning of the year, students had been asked to always turn off their cell phones during a class. The principal had even gone further and asked that they be kept out of sight. The principal's request was not being honored by many students. Up to now, all that Sean had done for a first offence was to give the student a warning. Although it was only October, he was already getting repeat offenders. Even though there was no penalty for these students in the handbook, he had sent them to in-school suspension for the remainder of the day. Sean had no idea how he would deal with them if they were sent to him for a third offense. It wouldn't have surprised him if this were to occur in the near future.

While the phone going off in class was the most common problem, he was beginning to hear about even more serious issues. All of new models allowed students to text message each other. This was happening in classes and would continue to occur as long as the phones were allowed in the classroom. Certainly a student sending or receiving messages could not be fully engaged in the activities of the class, and it would undoubtedly affect their concentration.

More serious than just communicating with a friend during class, would be students text messaging during an examination. There have always been ingenious ways to cheat on a test, but this technology would increase the need for vigilance of teachers proctoring an exam. Along with cheating, there have been students who have been guilty of criminal activity such as calling in a bomb threat. Even worse, it would be possible for a student to detonate a bomb using a cell phone. There also was the fact that public officials involved in crisis management were worried about messages going out of the school during an emergency that might create panic and disrupt and delay effective responses. In addition, cell phone use could overload the telephone systems and hamper the work of those officials dealing with the crisis.[1]

The newest potential problem was the camera phone, which would allow the owner to take pictures. Sean could imagine the problems caused by students using this option in a bathroom or locker room. He was not aware of this ever occurring in his school, but it was likely that even if it did happen, he would not know it. Given all of the potential trouble caused by cell phones, he thought it might be useful to raise the issue at the next meeting of the school administrative staff.

On the other hand, he knew that two years ago the school principal, Tara Snyder, his boss, had not been willing to adopt a definitive policy on the use of cell phones in school other than to discourage students from bringing them into class. Sean knew that her position had been affected by conversations with several parents. These individuals had expressed their appreciation that it was possible for their children to call them at any time. One of the parents' daughters had been the victim of bullying, and the parent was able to quickly intervene by calling an assistant principal. The parent reported the incident because the child was hesitant to do so. Although in this case, the phone had helped curtail bullying, Sean was aware that bullying or harassment threats also occurred by students using text messaging.

Another parent was grateful that it was so convenient to be able to talk to her son during the school day. Because her work schedule was unpredictable, she often needed her middle school child to go home right after school to babysit for his brother who was in the first grade. On other occasions, her son would call her to arrange transportation from after school activities. Sean was not aware of the degree of parental support for cell phones in schools, but a more restrictive policy could very well create serious opposition from some parents.

Although as an administrator he had begun to see cell phones as a bother, he had read an article in *Teaching Today* that said cell phones could be used for educational purposes. He decided to make a copy of the suggestions contained in the story. It read:

### Cell Phones as Teaching Tools:

- **Calculators.** Although most schools have them in math class, other classes that don't have them on hand for students can benefit from number crunching. For example, social studies students studying elections can quickly determine percentages of electoral votes or other scenarios. Science classrooms can use them to perform calculations related to fieldwork.
- **Digital cameras.** Not all schools or classrooms are outfitted with digital cameras, although many can benefit from them. For example, students can use them to document a variety of things for multimedia presentations or reports. Field trips can be documented and incorporated into digital travelogues.
- **Internet access.** Some phones have wireless Internet access, thus opening up a world of possibilities for class use. Science students might conduct fieldwork and submit their observations or data to either an internal or external data gathering site.
- **Dictionaries.** Students in literature and language arts classes can benefit from being able to quickly query the definition of a word. Additionally, students who are English learners especially can benefit from the translation dictionaries that are becoming available on cell phones.[2]

Because of these possibilities, as well as the public support of parents, the state legislatures in Michigan, Indiana, Georgia, and Illinois were considering laws to repeal their state bans on cell phones in schools. Even school administrators are not all agreed on what should be done. A spokesperson for the Association for School Administrators recently publicly admitted that allowing students to have cell phones in school, "can reassure families because they can be in touch with their children."[3]

The more he had read about the issue, the more concerned he became about developing a concise policy that would be overly restrictive. Even so, it seemed to him that the current lack of any specific rules made his job that much more difficult. He decided that he would make a list of the alternative policies that might be considered.

The most clear-cut solution would be to impose an outright ban on cell phones in the school. An appropriate immediate penalty might be the confiscation of the device. He wondered if such a penalty could be challenged and also how and when the phone would be returned to the student. Of course such a policy would also require that he develop consequences for repeat offenders.

Another possibility was to allow students to have them in school as long as they were not visible during a class. This would allow a student to carry them, but not to send or receive messages during a class. It would be acceptable to communicate before or after school as well as between classes. As long as students were allowed to have cell phones in the building, it was probable that students would still use them in class. He could hear a student now explaining how he had forgotten to turn off his phone before class. Allowing students to have the phone on their person would still leave open the possibility of text messaging or cheating if the teacher was not constantly on guard.

A more stringent option would be to allow students to keep their phone in their lockers and to use them only in the case of an emergency. This would eliminate the parents' ability to communicate with their children during the school day. Such an approach could also be extremely difficult to enforce.

A final alternative seemed to be to allow the students to have and use the devices freely in school and to only react when their use was unlawful or overtly disruptive. This approach would undoubtedly continue the parade of teacher referrals. If nothing else, he would at least like a written policy on the consequences of those students referred to him, especially any students who were guilty of a second or third offense. Personally, he had enjoyed the comment of one of his social studies teachers who had responded when a cell phone rang in his class, "If that's for me, tell them I'm busy teaching." Unfortunately, a teacher can't use this line every time it happens in the class.

If he wished to do anything, Sean had to decide whom to talk to first. There was the upcoming administrative meeting, but he was hesitant to spring this topic on his boss. He worried that if he talked to her before the meeting, she might discourage him from doing anything. The faculty, he expected, would support a tightening up of the policy, but he was not at all sure about the Board of Education. Having read the newspaper stories about the issue, he did not expect his state legislature to consider a statewide restrictive policy, so it would have to come at either the school district or individual school level.

## DISCUSSION QUESTIONS

1. Do you have sympathy with at least some parents for wanting to allow students to use their cell phones in school? Why or why not?
2. Are you worried about the potential problems these devices might cause in schools beyond the nuisance of interruptions during class? Why or why not?
3. If you were Sean, what, if anything, would you do about the cell phone problem in your school?

## NOTES

1. "School Safety: Cell Phones, Camera Phones, & Pagers," National School Safety and Security Services, http://www.schoolsecurity.org/trends/cell_phones.html. (Accessed March 21, 2007)

2. Elizabeth Melville, "Cell Phones: Nuisance or Necessity," *Teaching Today*, April 2006, http://www.glencoe.com/sec/teachingtoday/educationupclose.phtml/52. (Accessed March 21, 2007)

3. Ellen R. Delisio, "Schools, States Review Cell Phone Bans," *Education World*, February 7, 2002, http://www.education-world.com /a_issue/issues270.shtml. (Accessed March 21, 2007)

## ADDITIONAL RESOURCES

Dessoff, Alan 2005. "IPods OK in Class." *District Administration* 41(12). Retrieved April 21, 2007, from Professional Development Collection.

Dodds, Richard, and Christine Y. Mason. 2005. "Cell Phones and PDA's Hit K–6." *Communicator* 28: 1–2.

Kim, Sang H., Kerry Holmes, and Clif Mims. 2005. "Mobile Wireless Technology: Opening a Dialogue in the New Technologies in Education." *TechTrends* 49: 54–89.

Pickett, A. Dean, and Christopher Thomas. 2006. "Turn OFF that Phone." *American School Board Journal* 193(4). Retrieved April 21, 2007, from Professional Development Collection.

Scaccia, Jessie, and Elizabeth L. Ritter 2006. "Should Cell Phones Be Banned in Schools?" *New York Times Upfront* 137(7): 19. Retrieved April 21, 2007, from Professional Development Collection.

Schmit, Dan. 2007. "Creating a Broadcasting Empire..from the Corner of Your Classroom!" *Multimedia & Internet @ Schools* 14(1). Retrieved April 21, 2007, from Professional Development Collection.

"Should Cell Phones and Pagers Be Allowed in School?" 2001. *NEA Today* 19(6): 11.
    Smith, BetsAnn. 2000. "Quantity Matters: Annual Instruction Time in an Urban
    School System." *Educational Administration Quarterly* 3(5): 652–682.Sheekey,
    Arthur D. ed. 2003. *How to Ensure Ed/Tech is Not Oversold and Underused.* Lan-
    ham, Md.: Scarecrow Press.
"Should Cell Phones and Pagers Be Allowed in School?" 2001, March. *NEA Today*
    (6): 11. Retrieved April 21, 2007, from Professional Development Collection.
St. Gerard, Vanessa. 2006. "Updating Policy on Latest Risks for Students with Cell
    Phones in the School." *Education Digest* 72(4): 43–45.

*Case Study 22*

# Will More Time in School Really Make a Difference?

## extended school day

One of the recommendations in the *Nation at Risk* report in 1983 was to increase the amount of instructional time in our public schools. It pointed out that in England, it was not unusual for students to be in school eight hours a day for two hundred and twenty days while in the United States, it frequently was no more than six and a half hours for one hundred and eighty days. Although twenty years later, there has been an increase in daily schedules of forty percent in high schools, thirty percent in middle schools, and thirty-four percent in elementary schools, the amount of additional learning time has most often been minimal. It is also true that less than twenty percent of schools have created longer years. [1]

With the passage of the No Child Left Behind Act, states and individual school districts are revisiting this approach as a way to raise test scores. It has also become an issue in the congressional debate over the reauthorization of the law. Senator Ted Kennedy, one of the architects of the original law in 2002, is filing legislation to provide schools $50 million to help pay for increases in instructional time. His goal is to raise this amount to $150 million by 2012. [2] Because the initiative to increase instructional time is being discussed at every level of government, school administrators can expect to be dealing with the issue for years to come.

Superintendent Allison Hanson had not slept all that well after the Board of Education meeting last evening. The public portion of the agenda had gone well, but when the board adjourned for an executive session at the end of the meeting, a new issue arose. Once alone, the board members felt free to say exactly what was on their minds. The purpose of the executive session was to hold a preliminary discussion on the negotiations with the teachers' union, which were scheduled to begin in six weeks. With the end of a three-year contract only five months away, it was time to begin thinking about the proposals that the district would make during the talks.

The two newest members of the board had come to the meeting with a plan. Bob Barton and Ken Fuller were successful businessmen in the community who had been elected the previous spring. Ken was now retired but he had been president of the local chamber of commerce. The two men came to the meeting prepared with several articles to support their idea of an initiative to increase instructional time in the Linwood City Schools. Bob had done his homework and began his argument by reviewing the schedule of the school district. He started by pointing out that his son Rex was taking five academic classes. These classes each met for forty-five minutes a day, five days a week, thus the students were receiving just slightly more than three and a half hours of academic instruction during the school day.

In addition, he noted that his son was spending no more than three or four hours a week on all of his homework. At best, the average student was devoting approximately twenty hours a week for his courses in English, math, science, and social studies. He then calculated the time his son was spending as a member of the basketball team. With practice, games, and travel time, he was allotting as much time for his athletic pursuits as he was for all of his major subjects combined. He ended his remarks by saying, "there is something wrong with this picture."

Ken then took over by giving an analysis of the school calendar. He said that he had always thought that students were in classes for one hundred and eighty days. Last year, he had kept track and he pointed out to the entire board some facts that Allison already knew. Out of the hundred and eighty days, five days had been used for mandated examinations and regular classes were not held. On four additional days, the students were not in school because the teachers were having professional growth days or teacher conference days. There had also been several early dismissals for parent conferences or for inclement weather. In all, he believed that there had been only one hundred and seventy days when students were actually in classes. This did not count the classes that were missed for assemblies and field trips. He closed his remarks by suggesting that, "it doesn't take a rocket scientist to conclude that if we want to improve test scores, the students need to spend more time on their academic subjects."

Following these introductory comments, the two new board members continued by sharing an article that had been published by the National School Board Association. It dealt with the KIPP (Knowledge Is Power Program) Schools. At the time that the article was published, there were fifteen of these schools. Ten of them were charter schools. The students were primarily poor minority children who spent sixty percent more time in school than their peers. Their reading and math scores had increased twice as much as similar students who were attending schools for less time.[3] When another board member suggested that his kids would hate spending sixty percent more time in school, Ken and Bob were ready with an answer. They read from an article with the headline, "Extended School Days Get High Marks, Even from Kids."[4]

Without a pause Bob went on to talk about how in Massachusetts, New York, and Connecticut, the governors were recommending that funds be made available to help school districts extend their instructional times.[5] Before they could continue, the president of the board interrupted them to remind the new members that the purpose of the executive session was to talk about contract negotiations with the teachers. With that cue, Ken said that this was the reason they were raising the issue.

They believed that when the board went into negotiations with the faculty, they should tie any salary increases to either longer work days or a longer school year. It was his opinion that in the past, the district had given automatic teacher raises and had never gotten anything in return. As she looked around the room, it appeared to Allison that the two men had a receptive audience among the other board members. Because she did not feel ready to discuss the issue further, she promised the board to come back in two weeks with some thoughts on the proposal.

Sitting at her desk on the morning after the meeting, Allison was beginning to recognize a number of difficulties related to the board members' proposal. Prior to going to bed last evening she had gone online and read the *New York Times* article that had been referred to at the meeting. While doing so, she came across several letters to the editor that were written in reaction to the article. Having made a copy, she now read the letters for a second time.

To the Editor:

**Failing Schools See a Solution in Longer Day (March 26, 2007)**

Re "Failing Schools See a Solution in Longer Day" (front page, March 26):
When are they going to wake up and get it right? They can make the school day 24 hours if they like, and nothing will substantially change.
I taught elementary school for 30 years and noticed that as the school day progresses only one thing basically happens to kids: they get tired!
If you really want to improve public education, rather than increasing the length of the school day, it would be better to decrease class size. Teachers would then have more of a chance to administer individual instruction during class time, to all children. There wouldn't be many chances to tune out, and more work of real value would be accomplished.
Children need time to be children. They're not going to get it in a nine-hour school day.

Those who hate school will only hate it more. Most of the other children will be burned out by the time they reach high school. And when will there be time to do homework?

Kathleen Crisci
New York, March 26, 2007

To the Editor:

Lengthening the school day alone will not solve our educational problems. In confronting one of America's greatest challenges, we must use one of America's greatest resources, our unparalleled network of community-based organizations (many dedicated to providing quality after-school programming). In New York City, Mayor Michael R. Bloomberg not only extended daily classroom time for some students, but he also allocated up to $121 million annually for Out-of-School Time programs. This money will support more than 700 after-school programs that will serve more than 80,000 young people by September 2008.
A recent independent evaluation indicates that the city's system is meeting the needs of parents, who can choose the program that's right for their child, as well as students, who are establishing social and educational connections outside school.
It is time for federal and state education policy to reflect the fact that learning continues after the final bell rings.

Jeanne B. Mullgrav
New York, March 26, 2007
*The writer is commissioner of the New York City Department of Youth and Community Development.*[6]

Possibly the after-school program discussed in the second letter would be something that would be acceptable to the majority of the community. She had also read the previous evening that some of the districts that had established longer days had done so only for students who were having academic difficulties. To better organize her thoughts, she decided to list some of her concerns about the board members' proposals.

- Lengthening the school day at the high school level would undoubtedly interfere with the outside work schedules of many of the students. She knew that students would tell her that they needed to work as much as possible if they were going to afford college.
- The extracurricular program, especially interscholastic sports would also be affected. It could possibly result in students arriving home after 6 p.m. or

possibly coming back to school after supper for practices. Of course she could suggest to the coaches to shorten their practices, but she was sure that they would tell her that this would cause them to be less competitive with other schools.

- Lengthening the school year would also cut into family vacations.
- Although difficult to predict, she believed the response of parents would be mixed. For those with younger children, it might reduce the time they were alone after school and cut down on their child care costs. With older students it might help to get them off the streets.

Even though these were factors that had to be considered, she knew that the biggest problem would be with the teachers' union. The union would be unlikely to settle for less than a three percent raise without an increase in the time that they were expected to spend teaching. Depending on how much additional time was added to the schedule, the union would be seeking a raise in excess of the three percent to compensate them for extra work.

Even if the board was able to come up with additional funds for salaries, she was not sure how willing the teachers would be to negotiate seriously about this issue. Many of the younger faculty members had families, and one of the reasons they had gone into the profession was to be able to spend more time with their children. More than half of the Linwood teachers lived outside of the school district, and those with children in other schools would find it more difficult to coordinate their work schedules with their family obligations. It could even force them to pay for additional child care. Faculty members who were also coaches were already working very long days and forcing them to be in school longer could well lead some of them to decide that coaching was just taking too much time.

Even if there could be some agreement on adding instructional time to the schedule, there would have to be a well-constructed plan to ensure that the extra time was being well spent. It also occurred to her that changing the school schedule would have implications for the transportation department, office personnel, and even the custodial schedule. She thought about the possibility of having a conversation with the members of union leadership to seek out their thoughts, but such a private talk could be dangerous if adding time to the school day or year became a major issue in the upcoming negotiations.

In any case, she had to prepare herself to address the problem at the next board meeting. She could very well find that a majority of the board agreed with its two new members and that this issue could greatly impact the impending union talks.

## DISCUSSION QUESTIONS

1. Do you believe that lengthening the school day or year can positively impact student learning? Why or why not?
2. What reactions to this issue would you expect from students, parents, and teachers?
3. What strategy can school districts use to gain support of students, parents, nonteaching personnel, and teachers for increasing their school schedules?
4. What should Allison say to the Board of Education at the next meeting?

## NOTES

1. U.S. Department of Education, National Commission on Excellence in Education, *A Nation at Risk: The Imperative for Educational Reform*, April 1983.

2. James Vaznis, "Kennedy to Promote Extended School Days," *The Boston Globe*, January 8, 2007, http://www.boston.com/news/local/articles/2007/01/08/kennedy_to_promote_extended_school_days/?page=2. (Accessed March 29, 2007)

3. Ellie Ashford, "At KIPP Schools, More Time in School Translates into Higher Test Scores," *School Board News*, National School Boards Association, November 2002, http://nsba.org/site/doc_sbn.asp?TRACKID=VID=58&CID=314&DID=8190+. (Accessed March 15, 2007)

4. David Pomerantz, "Extended School Days Get High Marks, Even from Kids," *The Boston-Bay State Banner*, March 22, 2007, http://www.baystatebanner.com/issues/2007/03/22/news/local03220716.htm. (Accessed March 29, 2007)

5. Diana Jean Schemo, "Failing Schools See a Solution in Longer Day," *New York Times*, March 26, 2007, http://www.nytimes.com/2007/03/26/us/26schoolday.html. (Accessed March 30, 2007)

6. "A Longer Day for Schoolchildren?" Letters to the Editor, *New York Times,* March 30, 2007, http://www.nytimes.com/2007/03/30/opinion/130schools.html?_r=1&oref=slogin. (Accessed March 30, 2007)

## ADDITIONAL RESOURCES

Brown, Cynthia G. 2001. "Extended Learning: What Are the States Doing?" *Principal* 80(3): 12–15.

Dodd, Catherine, and Donald Wise. 2002. "Extended-Day Programs: Time to Learn." *Leadership* 32(1). National Education Commission on Time and Learning. 2000. *Prisoners of Time: Too Much to Teach, Not Enough Time to Teach It* (Expanded ed.). Peterborough, NH: Crystal Springs Books.

Owens, Dan, and Nancy Vallercamp. 2003. "Eight Keys to a Successful Expanded-Day Program." *Principal* 82(5): 22–25.

Woelfel, Kay. 2005. "Learning Takes Time for At-Riskers." *Principal* 85(2): 18–21.

*Case Study 23*

# How Can We Make Our Schools Secure?

*school security*

**Beginning with the Columbine massacre in April 1999 and now after the more recent tragedy at Virginia Tech, school security has been an issue for administrators at every level. As a result of community pressure and, in some cases, state mandates, schools have created plans aimed at providing a safe and orderly environment for their students. In addition, they have also had to consider ways to react in the event of a crisis. Some districts have spent large amounts of money on security hardware such as special lock systems and surveillance cameras. Across the country, many schools have hired police or specially trained school resource officers to assist administrators and faculty in enforcing school rules.**

**At the same time, other districts have done little more than to try to ensure that unauthorized persons not be allowed to wander freely in their buildings. Whatever steps a district may have taken to secure its schools, if an incident occurs in a community, or even in an area school, there will be a heightened awareness of the importance of a school safety plan.**

The newspaper had become interested in school security following a feature story about an incident at a high school that was adjacent to the Woodridge Central School District. During a recent school day, a twenty-two-year-old man had entered Linwood High School and somehow found and attacked a seventeen-year-old junior who attended the school. The student required hospitalization, and the attacker had been able to leave the school and was not apprehended until a student witness identified him, allowing the local police to make an arrest.

As a result of this incident, the daily newspaper in a nearby city decided to investigate security arrangements at local high schools. The plan was to have one of their young reporters test the systems. The first three schools that the reporter visited had at least identified her as a visitor, had her sign in, and wear a name tag. It looked as if these schools were doing a good job at monitoring visitors.

The reporter's last visit was to be to Woodridge High School. When she drove into the parking lot, she noticed that the door leading to the tennis courts was propped open. It appeared that there was a physical education class learning to play tennis, and it was possible that the instructor had chosen not to close the door when the group went outside. Taking advantage of this opportunity, the reporter walked into the main hall of the school building. For the next half hour, she made her way through the school. Many people were friendly with her and one student, and several adults asked her if they could help her find something. She saw several signs saying that visitors must report to the office, but she ignored them and walked through the cafeteria where students were having lunch.

It appeared that the adults working in the school were supposed to be wearing identification badges, but she noticed that there were many who did not at least have them where they could be seen. Following her stroll through the cafeteria, she passed by the main entrance, where she saw a woman at a table with a sign-in book and some visitor nametags. The reporter walked past the table, and the woman never seemed to notice her. Not once during her time in the building did anyone challenge her for not having a nametag.

Returning to the newspaper office, the young woman wrote a front-page story about the lack of security at Woodridge High School. When the article was brought to his attention, the high school principal, Ron Stanford, felt both humiliated and angry. The school had the normal security arrangements. All of the building's eight exterior doors, except the main entrance were to be kept locked. During the school day, there was always a staff member at the main entrance who would stop and question anyone entering the building. If they had a legitimate reason for being in the school, visitors would sign the book, noting the time and the purpose of the visit. They would then be given a visitor's badge to wear. Administrators, faculty, and nonteaching staff were to wear an identification badge at all times.

Ron had to admit that the badge rule was not always strictly enforced. The fact was that he was sometimes guilty himself of forgetting his badge. The same was true of a number of the faculty and staff. As the principal of the building, he knew that he was responsible for the lax enforcement of the security rules and therefore decided to make a concerted effort to strengthen the program.

When he first read the article, Ron had considered calling up the reporter and complaining about the fact that she had sneaked in the building, but on further consideration, he knew that the door should have been locked. The day after the story appeared in the newspaper, he called a special meeting of all faculty and staff to emphasize the importance of building security. He even made an extended announcement over the public address system for students, asking their help in identifying any unauthorized visitors to the building. After taking these steps, he called the reporter and instead of complaining, thanked her for raising the issue. He told her what he had done and suggested that, in the future, the building would be secure.

Several weeks went by, and the whole matter seemed to fade from everyone's consciousness. The fact was that, in his three years as high school principal, with the exception of several bomb scares, there had been no serious security problems at Woodridge High School. Although the school had gone on to new problems, the newspaper editor had not forgotten the issue. One day, he drove by the school and noticed that the back door at the loading dock was wide open and no one seemed to be around. This time, he assigned a young male reporter to attempt to use this door to gain entrance to the building. Without incident, the young man walked into the school and was not challenged by anyone. He had been told to check whether the adults were wearing the required badges and during his visit he saw three individuals who had no badge showing. Like his colleague, he too moved through the building without being challenged.

His story appeared the next day under the headline, "Security Remains Lax at Woodridge." The next morning, Ron was summoned to the superintendent's office where the first words of his boss were, "I thought you solved this problem." He was told that he was to do whatever was necessary to deal with this issue.

During the next several days, he spent hours reading about possible ways to make schools more secure. Ron even called up several fellow principals to find out what they were doing. Because some of the possibilities included some construction to create a more secure entrance to the building, he even contacted an architect friend to talk about the potential cost of such a project. With every alternative he considered, there seemed to be major expenses involved. After doing this initial research, he had boiled down the possibilities.

- The district could hire security guards. Some schools had signed agreements with the local police to provide an officer in the building during the school day.
- A whole new category of security personnel has emerged in recent years. Called school resource officers, these individuals are not part of a police force, but rather are specially trained staff whose work is confined to security in schools.
- Some schools have included a keyless entry lock system with a proximity reader to discourage teachers from propping a door open.
- Other schools have placed security cameras in strategic areas of the building.

Knowing there may well be other alternatives, Ron was thinking of the possibility of recommending to his superintendent that a districtwide committee be formed to consider these and other options. Certainly, there were many people in the community and possibly within the school, who knew a lot more about the problem than he could learn in the few days before the next board meeting.

## DISCUSSION QUESTIONS

1. If Ron were allowed to establish a safety committee to make recommendations on how to better secure the building, what type of representation might such a committee have?
2. Do you feel that most communities would support significant expenditures for additional school security? Why or why not?
3. How should Ron react to his superintendent's request that he quickly solve the problem?

## ADDITIONAL RESOURCES

Allen, Melissa, and Betty Y. Ashbaker. 2004. "Strengthening Schools: Involving Paraprofessionals in Crisis Prevention and Intervention." *Intervention in School and Clinic* 39(3): 139–146.

Axelman, Michael J. 2006. "African American Youth Speak Out about the Making of Safe High Schools." *Preventing School Failure* 50(4): 37–44.

Bucher, Katherine T., and M. Lee Manning. 2003. "Challenges and Suggestions for Safe Schools." *Clearing House* 76: 160–164.

Frattaroli, Shannon, and John S. Vernick. 2006. "Separating Batterers and Guns: A Review and Analysis of Gun Removal Laws in 50 States." *Evaluation Review* 30: 296–312.

Heinen, Ethan, Jaci Webb-Dempsey, Lucas C. Moore, Craig S. McClellan, and Carl H. Friebel. 2006. "Implementing District Safety Standards at the Site Level." *NAASP Bulletin* 90: 207–220.

Hunnicutt, Susan. 2006. *School Shootings.* Farmington Hills, MI: Greenhaven Press/Thomson Gale.

MacKay, A. Wayne, and Janet Burt-Gerrans. 2005. "Student Freedom of Expression: Violent Content and the Safe School Balance." *McGill Journal of Education*, 40: 423–443.

Merrow, John 2004. "Safety and Excellence. Safety in the Schools." *Educational Horizons* 83(1): 19–32.

Quinn, Terrence. (2002). "The Inevitable School Crises: Are You Ready?" *Principal* 81(5): 6–8.

Torres, Mario S., Jr., and Yihsuan Chen. 2006. "Assessing Columbine's Impact on Students' Fourth Amendment Case Outcomes: Implications for Administrative Discretion and Decision Making." *NAASP Bulletin* 90 185–206.

## Case Study 24

# Are School Librarians Becoming Obsolete?

## personnel questions

The issue came up during a public discussion at the Board of Education meeting. Ken MacIntyre was a retired businessman who believed that schools should be run like a business. During his sixteen years as a member of the Fairwood Board of Education, he had made numerous suggestions as to how the school district could save money. Because he was retired, more than any other board member, he took the time to study carefully the school budget. As chairperson of the board budget committee, he saw it as his personal mission to find ways to reduce expenditures and, if possible, lower the property tax rate.

The discussion began when Ken asked how many retirements were likely to occur among the professional faculty at the end of the school year. Because the contract with the professional employees called for those planning to retire to notify the superintendent no later than March 1, a list of retirements had already been prepared. Two of the names on the list were those of school librarians in the district. Upon learning this, he asked whether any of the other three librarians would be retiring in the near future. The superintendent suggested that two additional librarians would be eligible to retire within the next three years and that they were likely to retire within that period.

After hearing the names of the two librarians on the list, Ken introduced his plan. It was his opinion that it was unnecessary for the district to have five certified librarians. He went on to suggest that the retiring librarians could be replaced by a different kind of employee. On a recent tour of the school libraries, he had noticed that in all of them, most of the students were using the computers and almost none were reading books. As in the computer labs, it seemed to him that the library could easily be supervised by an aide who was perhaps a two-year graduate of the community college. Such a person could have majored in computer science and could be very helpful to the students.

He also pointed out that the circulation desk and card catalogue were now computerized.

Ken admitted that when he visited the libraries, he observed the librarians meeting and reading to a group of children, but this too was a task that could be undertaken by an aide. He suggested that because teacher aides read to children in the classroom, they certainly could do so in the library. It surely did not take someone with a master's degree to read a children's book to a group of elementary students.

Turning to the secondary schools, he had talked to his nephew who was a social studies teacher in another district. This young teacher had told him that most students use the Internet to find sources for any research projects they were assigned. Only recently had the young man's social studies department mandated that students use at least some sources from books. In his school now, one-third of all research had to be done with print sources. In any case, Ken was convinced that any well-trained library clerk could help students find books on the topics they were researching. He also had learned that at the public library, many of the staff were not certified librarians.

He even thought of a historical precedent for his plan. As a veteran board member, he remembered when the school had gone from certified school nurse teachers to registered nurses. The registered nurses, many of whom had not even gained a bachelor's degree, were paid one-third less than the school nurse teachers, saving the district a considerable amount of money. This personnel change had also come at a time when the school nurse teachers were retiring. Jane Hatcher, who was also a veteran board member, felt it was necessary to point out that school nurse teachers were not really needed in the classroom any longer when schools were able to hire certified health teachers.

This interruption did not seem to deter Ken as he was ready to summarize his plan. The goal was to replace the two retiring librarians with well-trained teacher assistants at approximately one-third of the salaries of the individuals who were leaving. When the next two librarians retired, he would recommend the same course of action. He conceded that the district should always maintain one professional librarian to act as an administrator. This individual would be responsible for training the aides and the overall administration of the five libraries. In addition the professional librarian would be expected to prepare the district library budget and order new materials.

According to his calculations, when fully implemented, the proposal could save the district tens of thousands of dollars in personnel costs. When he had finished his remarks, the superintendent thanked him for his ideas and promised that the school administration would study the proposal and report back at the next meeting.

Assistant Superintendent Tracy Keller knew that it was likely to be her responsibility to do some homework regarding the issue. She was right. The next morning, the superintendent suggested that she prepare a draft document responding to the board member's proposal. This draft would be placed on the agenda of the next meeting of the school administrative team.

Because the idea had been shared publicly, Tracy was not surprised that within three days she received a position paper from the district's five librarians listing their concerns about the proposal. The document was fifteen pages long, and Tracy had chosen to summarize the arguments for her own use. For her at least, these were the important points made by the position paper.

- Our school librarians are all currently experts in the use of technology. For certified librarians trained during the past twenty years, the use of the computer as a tool has been a prominent aspect of their education. The older librarians employed by the district had taken advantage of numerous in-service opportunities and had learned on the job. In fact, the five librarians working for the district had introduced and implemented computer use in the school libraries. Their knowledge went far beyond that of a two-year computer science graduate of a community college. Most important, they had learned to evaluate Internet sites so that they could assist students to choose research sources wisely.
- Librarians currently played a prominent role in encouraging students to read books during their free time. The report cited a reading program that rewarded students who kept track of the books that they read over the summer. As part of such a program, parents were asked to verify that their children had read the books. Prizes had been given for students who read the most. The elementary libraries opened several days during the summer so that students could return and sign out books. Librarians had done this without asking to be compensated.

  One librarian had gained a grant that allowed children to talk by telephone with famous children's authors. The students read books by the authors and prepared questions to ask during a forty-five-minute conference call with the author. Activities such as these were instrumental in encouraging students to read outside the school. Such efforts could only help with reading scores in the district.

  As far as having library assistants read to students visiting the school library, a key component of such an activity was choosing the best children's literature available. Professional librarians were trained to know and to keep abreast of the best children's literature. It was also true, the report noted, that librarians not only read to the students, but engaged them in meaningful discussions about the book. This indeed was teaching, and computer science graduates were not trained to use literature as a teaching tool.

- If books in libraries are being underused, the blame should not be placed solely on librarians. Too many teachers were not taking advantage of their school libraries. Several younger teachers, especially in areas such as social studies and English, have gone through college using the Internet as their primary research source. Teachers need to be encouraged to give assignments that mandate that students use a variety of sources.

- If we want children to practice reading, books and magazines are a better source than reading a computer screen. Because we do not allow students to make unlimited copies of sources from the Internet, they often tend only to skim the Web sites that they are using. They pick out a bit of information or quotation and move on. This is different from sitting in a comfortable chair with a book or a magazine where a student might well do more in-depth reading. Also, students do not read from a computer screen for pleasure. Literature contained in a book is a positive form of recreation that not only improves our skills, but enriches our lives. The goal of schools should be to make students lifelong readers. If we can create this interest in our students, we will broaden them as human beings and as citizens.

- Principals and other administrators can also be helpful by encouraging teachers to work with the school librarian. If teacher evaluations included a category dealing with how teachers are encouraging students to read books and periodicals, perhaps faculty members would seek to find ways to motivate the students to read and to vary their research sources.

- The position paper also admitted that librarians needed to better communicate to principals and teachers their activities and ideas for increasing traditional library usage. It acknowledged that they need to become more active and involved in curriculum projects and in efforts to communicate more effectively with faculty members. Like every other teacher, they needed to become engaged in helping the school meet the challenges of No Child Left Behind. This is especially true in the area of language arts.

As she read over her notes, Tracy was impressed by some of the arguments contained in the position paper. She was doubtful whether Ken would feel the same. Her mind turned to some practical questions related to the issue. She remembered that there were already some aides in the library. Often two adults were assigned to a library. Although the district used some unpaid volunteers, she was sure that some of these aides were on the district payroll. She needed to check their qualifications and their job descriptions. In any case, a second person was probably necessary if the library was to be open all day and after school.

In addition, she was aware that although the current experienced librarians might have a salary close to sixty thousand dollars per year, a more recent graduate of a library science program might be paid thirty-five thousand. This being the case, a change to a community college graduate might only save the district fifteen thousand dollars a year.

With all of these things to consider, Tracy would have to somehow put together a report for the upcoming administrative meeting. She suspected that during this period of tight school budgets, the superintendent might have some sympathy with the board member's suggestion. Thinking that she might well be becoming overly conservative, she had to admit to herself that she was not convinced that school librarians were obsolete.

## DISCUSSION QUESTIONS

1. Do you think the board member's suggestion is a good way to reduce the school district's personnel budget? Why or why not?
2. Prepare a list of arguments you might use to support the board member's idea.
3. Prepare a list of arguments you would use to oppose the recommendation.
4. Given the fact that the district currently has three elementary, one middle school, and one high school library, is there any possible compromise available to the district? What is it? Would you support a compromise?
5. If you were Tracy, what would be the nature of your report for the administrative meeting?

## ADDITIONAL RESOURCES

Barack, Lauren. 2006."Libraries Obsolete?" *School Library Journal* 52(9): 26.

Buzzeo, Toni. 2007. "Literacy and the Changing Role of the Elementary Library Media Specialist." *Library Media Connection* 25(7): 18–19.

Cart, Michael. 2007. "Teacher-Librarian as Literacy Leader." *Teacher Librarian* 34(3): 8–12.

Eisenberg, Michael B. 2006. "Three Roles for the 21st-Century Teacher-Librarian." *CSLA Journal* 29(2): 21–23.

Geitgey, Gayle, and Ann E. Tepe. 2007. "Can You Find the Evidence-Based Practice in Your School Library?" *Library Media Connection* 25(6): 10–12.

Jurkowski, Odin L. 2006. "The Library as a Support System for Students." *Intervention in School & Clinic* 42(2): 78–83.

Loertscher, David. 2006. "Gauging the Impact of Teacher and Teacher-Librarian Collaboration." *Teacher Librarian* 34(2): 41.

Loertscher, David. 2006. "What Flavor Is Your School Library? The Teacher-Librarian as Learning Leader." *Teacher Librarian* 34(2): 8–12.

Oberg, Dianne. 2006. "Developing the Respect and Support of School Administrators." *Teacher Librarian* 33(3): 13–18.

# We Can't Just Kick Him Out

## discipline and students with special needs

The 1975 passage of the federal legislation known as Public Law 94–142, the Education for All Handicapped Children Act has brought about dramatic changes in our public schools. Since it was first passed, it has been amended several times, including the 1990 law, which is called the Individuals with Disabilities Education Act (IDEA). The law was also reauthorized with some changes in 1997 and 2004. In the hearings for the original 1975 law, members of Congress learned that, "1.75 million children with disabilities were excluded from school and another four million were not receiving full educational services."[1] The legislation stated that students should be placed in the "least restrictive environment," which is to say that whenever possible, children should not be placed in self-contained special education classes, but rather they should be assigned to regular classrooms. The requirement for school districts to do this has been labeled "inclusion." The wording in the Individuals with Disabilities Education Act states that:

> to the maximum extent appropriate, handicapped children, including children in public or private institutions, or other care facilities, are to be educated with children who are not handicapped, and that special classes, separate schooling, or the removal of handicapped children from the regular educational environment shall only occur when the nature or severity of the handicap is such that education in regular classes with the use of supplementary aids and services cannot be achieved satisfactorily.[2]

Many students with serious disabilities have been placed in regular classrooms. This practice has required numerous federal and state regulations that must be followed by school administrators.

Even prior to the formal hearing, the superintendent had said to Gloria Newman, a newly hired pupil personnel director in the district, that, "we've got to get that kid out of the school." The boy in question, Jimmy Sherman, was only ten years old and had been a student at William McKinley Elementary School for just six months. During this period he had spent numerous hours in in-school suspension for inappropriate behavior. His teacher, although she was very fond of the boy, was having difficulty controlling him. The school principal, Sidney Lewis, wasn't doing much better.

When Jimmy's family moved to the district, the boy had come with the special education designation of emotionally disturbed. He was taking medicine to help control his behavior, but his teacher was concerned that he often did not take the medicine. Because of his parents' insistence in the previous district, the boy has been placed in a regular fourth-grade classroom. When he moved to the Lakewood School District, the committee on special education decided to follow the same pattern. The fact that his current teacher was certified both as an elementary and a special education teacher caused the committee to assign several students with special education needs to her room each year.

Prior to developing the boy's Individualized Education Plan (IEP), Gloria Newman, who was also chairperson of the district committee on special education, called her counterpart in Jimmy's previous school. Among other things she learned was that Jimmy's parents also had a history of mental health problems. The entire family had been under the care of mental health authorities in the county where they had previously lived.

The current crisis was precipitated by Jimmy at the William McKinley Elementary School where he had caused a bomb scare in the building. There had been a number of similar events in neighboring schools, but this was the first one at an elementary school. Administrators in the area were showing "zero tolerance" for any student who was guilty of causing a bomb scare. In all of the recent cases, the students who had been involved had been suspended for the remainder of the school year.

Jimmy had confessed to his principal that he had written with a magic marker on the bathroom wall that there was a bomb in the building. As a result, Sidney suspended him for five days. This was the maximum suspension without a formal superintendent's hearing. On receiving the report of the incident, Joel Van Patten, the superintendent, informed Gloria and Sidney that he wanted to have a hearing on the fifth day of Jimmy's suspension and that the hearing was likely to end in a suspension for the remainder of the school year. Joel instructed Gloria to immediately begin looking for "a new and more appropriate placement for the boy."

Even before she left the superintendent's office, Gloria told her boss that such a penalty might not be possible because of the state regulations concerning the disciplining of students with disabilities. On hearing this, the superintendent said to Gloria, "I'm sure you can find a way." After leaving the superintendent, Gloria returned to her office and reviewed the appropriate regulations. She found the section that seemed to fit this set of circumstances.

The relevant wording dealt with the need to create a "manifestation team" to "review the relationship between the student's disability and the behavior subject to disciplinary action, to determine if the conduct is a manifestation of the disability." Further down in the policy it stated that:

> The manifestation team shall review all relevant information in the student's file . . . and any relevant information provided by the parents to determine if . . . the conduct in question was caused by or had a direct and substantial relationship to the student's disability.[3]

The regulations went on to state that if, in the view of this committee, the student's behavior resulted because of his or her disability, the student could not be permanently suspended or removed from his or her current placement, without a parent's permission. Gloria knew that the parents would want the boy returned to class, as they had grown to like and respect his teacher.

When the hearing for Jimmy was convened in the superintendent's office, those in attendance, along with the superintendent, included Jimmy, his parents, Sidney, Gloria, the school counselor, and Jimmy's teacher. In addition, the superintendent's administrative assistant was there to take minutes of the hearing. After the superintendent explained the purpose of the meeting, he asked the boy if he had written the note about the bomb on the wall of the boy's lavatory. Jimmy admitted that he had done so, and Joel then questioned him as to why he did it. After a long pause, Jimmy answered, "I am not sure, but I guess it was a voice I heard in my head that told me to do it."

Following this exchange, Joel asked his parents if they had any comments regarding their son's behavior. Jimmy's mother told the superintendent that they had run out of his medicine at the time of the incident but that they now had a new batch and that they also had made an appointment with the county Mental Health Department. They were sure that once they had his medicine regulated that he would be fine. They said they were sure that this kind of thing would not happen again, and they asked that Jimmy be given another chance and be allowed to return to class. At that point in the proceedings, Gloria noticed that the boy's teacher was wiping a tear from her eyes. There was no question that this situation was affecting her.

The hearing lasted less than ten minutes, and as it was concluded, Joel told the parents that he would call them later in the day with his decision. Gloria called a special meeting of the district committee on special education to act as the "manifestation team" which was required by the regulations. That meeting was scheduled to begin in just twenty minutes. As she was leaving the superintendent's conference room, Gloria shared with Joel her opinion that the boy was obviously mentally ill and that this was also the opinion of the school psychologist who would be a key participant in the upcoming meeting.

Despite these concerns, it was obvious that Joel had not changed his mind. That was made clear when he said to Gloria, "I don't care how much a new placement costs, you need to find a way. The parents are not going to fight us in court, and I know that the William McKinley Elementary School will be a safer place without him." On her way out the door, Gloria could not help but say to her boss, "You know Joel, we can't just kick him out."

## DISCUSSION QUESTIONS

1. Are you supportive of the concept of inclusive education for all students who require special education services? Why or why not?
2. How should Gloria deal with this issue in her meeting with the committee on special education?
3. If the committee decides to send the boy back to his current classroom, what should Gloria say to her superintendent?
4. Could Gloria have dealt with this matter differently prior to the hearing? What might she have done?

## NOTES

1. John D. Pulliam, and James J. Van Patten, *History of Education in America* (Upper Saddle River, New Jersey: Prentice Hall, 1995), 227.

2. Joel Spring, *American Education* (Boston, Massachusetts: McGraw-Hill, 2008), 110.

3. New York State Education Department, *Procedural Safeguards for Students with Disabilities Subject to Discipline*, January 2007, http://www.vesid.nysed.gov/specialed/publications/lawsandregs/part201.htm. (Accessed April 23, 2007)

## ADDITIONAL RESOURCES

*The complete learning disabilities directory, 2006/07.* 2006. Millerton, NY: Grey House.

Goldstein, Lisa. 2003. "Discipline Split at Heart of IDEA Overhaul Debate." *Education Week* 22(41): 1–3.

Krank, H. Mark, Charles E. Moon, and Gary F. Render. 2002. "Inclusion and Discipline Referrals." *Rural Educator* 24: 13–17.

Munn, Pamela, and Gwynedd Lloyd. 2005. "Exclusion and Excluded Pupils." *British Educational Research Journal* 31: 205–221.

Soodak, Leslie C. 2003. "Classroom Management in Inclusive Settings." *Theory Into Practice* 42: 327–333.

# We Need to Get Serious about Protecting the Environment

## *school and community relations*

Schools are expected to set an example in their community by doing things that are in the public interest. Today, there is ample reason to believe that there is a need to become more concerned about preserving the earth's natural resources. One national environmental group has stated the problem as follows:

> According to the U.S. Census Bureau, the world population is expanding at a mind-boggling rate. The world reached 1 billion people in 1800; 2 billion by 1922; and over 6 billion by 2000. It is estimated that the population will swell to over 9 billion by 2050. That means that if the world's natural resources were evenly distributed, people in 2050 will only have 25% of the resources per capita that people in 1950 had.
>
> The world has a fixed amount of natural resources—some of which are already depleted. So as population growth greatly strains our finite resources, there are fewer resources available. If we intend to leave our children and grandchildren with the same standard of living we have enjoyed, we must preserve the foundation of that standard of living.[1]

School administrators are expected to take a leading role in these environmental efforts. The fact is that a superintendent or principal cannot simply send out an e-mail and expect that the entire school community will respond appropriately. There needs to be a comprehensive educational program that will impact not only school employees, but students and parents. Even that is not enough as it will be necessary for the district to budget funds for any environmental initiative. The success of any such effort depends on the leadership provided.

Superintendent Anita Carson watched a television program the prior evening on global warming. The first thing that morning, she called her assistant superintendent, Ben Schultz, into her office to talk about the television program.

Following a detailed description of the environmental issues raised by the broadcast, she told Ben that he needed to come up with a plan to ensure that the East Iroquois Central School District was doing its part to save the environment. She said that, "We're already making some efforts, but we need to do more."

As the only assistant superintendent in the district, Ben was used to being given a wide variety of assignments. In his three years in his present position, he had never been given a task for which he was less well-prepared. As an English major in college, he had only taken two science courses and that had been twenty-five years ago. At the same time, he was not unaware of the global warming issue and the need for people to become involved in recycling programs. He had meant to see Al Gore's film, "An Inconvenient Truth," but had missed it when it played at the local theater. Perhaps it was already out on DVD, and he could rent it. As he began to think about his new assignment, Ben had to admit that he was not even sure what was happening in the various school district buildings in regard to recycling or any other environmental program.

After returning to his office, he spent the morning on the Internet and found out that school districts throughout the nation were undoubtedly ahead of the East Iroquois Central School District. The importance of doing more was brought home to him when he read an article titled, "Why Start in Schools?" This particular story impressed him so much that he took the following notes:

> Schools represent a large sector of the waste producers in this country, and they are typically some of the larger institutions in every municipality. If schools embrace environmentally responsible behaviors, there will be an immediate impact on its community's contribution to the local landfill. . . . Schools that model and teach principles of environmentally responsible behaviors to students will have a long-term impact. Teachers and parents are working everyday to educate the next generation of business owners and government officials. We can equip them with the knowledge and skills they will need in the future to manage the complexities of the environmental impact inherent in all activities. . . . Schools will serve as a catalyst for the community at large. . . . Parents who see recycling in the classrooms often report reinforcing that behavior at home, and working to institute recycling at work, as well.[2]

Although the efforts of schools can be significant, Ben was concerned about another statement that was contained in a second article. It read as follows:

> The sad truth, with some notable exceptions, is that most school waste reduction initiatives fail over time. The main reason is because these programs never were "institutionalized" by the adoption of formal resource conservation and environmentally preferable purchasing policies and operating procedures by

the local school board and the superintendent. Programs initiated by well-meaning teachers, principals, students, and other individuals generally disappear when these motivated individuals graduate, are promoted, or leave the school district.[3]

The same article included a list of five sources for sample school environmental policies. Ben instructed his administrative assistant to begin to search for as many sample school district policies as possible.

When he first began his reading, Ben had been thinking primarily about a comprehensive recycling program. The more he read, the clearer it become that there was much more required than just recycling. Many schools were heavily involved in attempting to reduce energy consumption. Such efforts included not only the question of heating their buildings, but also dealt with their transportation departments. Other efforts considered the toxicity of pesticides used on the school grounds. There were also initiatives to encourage increased carpooling by students and staff.

Just as he was attempting to learn as much as possible himself, it occurred to Ben that an essential aspect of any environmental initiative was education. This educational effort would involve the whole school community. He made a list of those who would have to become more knowledgeable in this area.

1. The school administration
2. The Board of Education
3. The faculty
4. The custodians
5. The cafeteria workers
6. The office personnel
7. The bus drivers
8. The students
9. The parents

If any program was going to be successful, it would require the support of all of these groups.

Also, there were certainly people with some background in these issues among each of the groups that he had listed. He thought first about the faculty where, especially in the science department, there might be those who were not only knowledgeable, but who also might have a high level of interest and commitment. Among the students, Ben was sure that at the high school there already was an ecology club. Certainly there were parents with special expertise in environmental issues. Very likely, there were also community members, who were not parents, but might be willing to become involved in establishing new policies.

Another aspect of the issue that was causing him concern was whether it was better to start small with a single initiative or to develop a comprehensive environmental program. It was possible that, for the coming year, the district could concentrate on establishing an effective recycling program. By itself, this would require the purchase of bins for collecting the materials and ensuring that the custodial personnel were given time to empty the containers and possibly transport the waste. A specific policy would have to be developed and an educational effort would have to be made to convince everyone connected with the school to participate. Such an effort would have to include the school cafeteria, which was the source of much of the waste created by the district. Recycling could also involve the district in a plan that included composting.

Of course recycling would only be one aspect of a total program. If he were to try to do more, it might well be necessary to create a districtwide task force to come up with a plan as well as the policies needed to implement it. Involving a lot of different people would have the advantage of gaining additional support for a broad-based approach. If he decided to move in this direction, he undoubtedly would have to convince his boss that the district would need some time to do the job right. In making the decision of what to do next, Ben knew that his goal should be more than the immediate satisfaction of the superintendent. He needed to think about what was right and what might be successful in the long run.

## DISCUSSION QUESTIONS

1. How can a school district go about trying to educate its entire community on the importance of conserving the earth's environment?
2. If the district decides to consider a comprehensive program in this area, how should they proceed in making such an initiative a reality?
3. If a task force on the environment is created, who should be asked to participate?
4. What should Ben do in regard to the superintendent's request?

## NOTES

1. "What's the Problem?" *Go Green Initiative*, 2007, http://gogreeninitiative.org/content/whygogreen/. (Accessed April 25, 2007)
2. "Why Start in Schools?" *Go Green Initiative*, 2007, http://gogreeninitiative.org/content/WhyGoGreen/WhyStartInSchools.html. (Accessed April 25, 2007)

3. Marshalle Graham, "District Administration," *California Integrated Waste Management Board*, 2006, http://www.ciwmb.ca.gov/schools/wastereduce/admin/. (Accessed April 25, 2007)

## ADDITIONAL RESOURCES

Potter, John F. 1996. "The Greening of Education: An Environmental Responsibility." *Environmentalist* 16(2): 79–82.

New York State Department of Environmental Education. (n.d.). *Green Schools*. http://www.dec.state.ny.us/website/dshm/redrecy/greenschools.html#ed. (Accessed April 28, 2007)

Skumatz, Lisa A., and John Green. 2001. "Evaluating the Impact of Recycling Education." *Resource Recycling* 20(8): 31–32, 34, 36–37.

# About the Author

**Bill Hayes** has been a high school social studies teacher, department chair, assistant principal, and high school principal. From 1973 to 1994, he served as superintendent of schools for the Byron-Bergen Central School District, which is located eighteen miles west of Rochester, NY. During his career, he was an active member of the New York State Council of Superintendents and is the author of a council publication, *The Superintendency: Thoughts for New Superintendents*, which is used to prepare new superintendents in New York State.

Mr. Hayes has also written a number of articles for various educational journals. After retiring from the superintendency he served as chair of the Teacher Education Division at Roberts Wesleyan College in Rochester until 2003. He currently remains a full-time teacher at Roberts Wesleyan. During the past seven years he has written ten books all published by Scarecrow Education Press and R&L Education. They include *Real-Life Case Studies for School Administrators, Real-Life Case Studies for Teachers, So You Want to be a Superintendent?, So You Want to be a School Board Member?, Real-Life Case Studies for School Board Members, So You Want to Become a College Professor?, So You Want to Become a Principal?, Are We Still a Nation at Risk Two Decades Later? Horace Mann's Vision of the Public Schools: Is it Still Relevant,? and The Progressive Education Movement: Is it Still a Factor in Today's Schools?*